# A WORKBOOK YOUR MIND U SILVA'S METHOD

## Achieve Your Mental Freedom with Simple Exercises from The Most Powerful Book Written for The Human Brain

OMA International Publications

© **Copyright 2023 - All rights reserved.**

The content contained within this book may not be reproduced, duplicated or transmitted without direct written permission from the author or the publisher.

Under no circumstances will any blame or legal responsibility be held against the publisher, or author, for any damages, reparation, or monetary loss due to the information contained within this book. Either directly or indirectly.

**Legal Notice:**

This book is copyright protected. This book is only for personal use. You cannot amend, distribute, sell, use, quote or paraphrase any part, or the content within this book, without the consent of the author or publisher.

**Disclaimer Notice:**

Please note the information contained within this document is for educational and entertainment purposes only. All effort has been executed to present accurate, up to date, and reliable, complete information. No warranties of any kind are declared or implied. Readers acknowledge that the author is not engaging in the rendering of legal, financial, medical or professional advice. The content within this book has been derived from various sources. Please consult a licensed professional before attempting any techniques outlined in this book.

By reading this document, the reader agrees that under no circumstances is the author responsible for any losses, direct or indirect, which are incurred as a result of the use of information contained within this document, including, but not limited to, — errors, omissions, or inaccuracies.

# Table of Contents

**INTRODUCTION** .................................................................................. 1

**CHAPTER 1** ........................................................................................ 5
INTRODUCTION TO THE SILVA METHOD ............................................... 5
   1.1 History and Development of The Silva Method by Jose Silva ..... 7
   1.2 Overview of The Silva Method: Potential and Goals ................. 10
   1.3 The Untapped Power of the Mind and How to Access It .......... 13

**CHAPTER 2** ...................................................................................... 18
UNDERSTANDING YOUR MIND: CONSCIOUS AND SUBCONSCIOUS ......... 18
   2.1 Defining Conscious and Subconscious Minds .......................... 19
   2.2 The Interaction Between the Conscious and Subconscious Minds ........................................................................................... 22
   2.3 Accessing the Power of the Conscious and Subconscious Minds ................................................................................................... 28

**CHAPTER 3** ...................................................................................... 32
IGNITING IMAGINATION AND VISUALIZATION ...................................... 32
   3.1 The Power of Imagination and Visualization ............................ 33
   3.2 Practical Exercises for Igniting Your Imagination ..................... 37
   3.3 Applying Visualization Techniques in Daily Life ...................... 41

**CHAPTER 4** ...................................................................................... 45
CORE PRINCIPLES OF THE SILVA METHOD ........................................... 45
   4.1 Foundational Principles of The Silva Method .......................... 46
   4.2 Understanding and Applying These Principles ....................... 49
   4.3 Case Studies of Effective Use of The Silva Method ................. 52

**CHAPTER 5** ...................................................................................... 56
THE POWER OF POSITIVE AFFIRMATIONS ............................................ 56
   5.1 Understanding the Role of Affirmations in Shaping Reality ..... 57
   5.2 How to Use Positive Affirmations for Maximum Effect ........... 59
   5.3 Case Studies and Success Stories ............................................ 63

## CHAPTER 6 ............................................................................................. 67

### SHAPING YOUR BELIEF SYSTEM .............................................................. 67
6.1 How Beliefs Shape Experiences ............................................. 68
6.2 Identifying Negative Thought Patterns and Limiting Beliefs .... 71
6.3 Techniques for Replacing Negative Thoughts with Positive Ones ............................................................................................ 74

## CHAPTER 7 ............................................................................................. 77

### ENTERING THE ALPHA STATE OF MIND ................................................... 77
7.1 Understanding the 'Alpha State of Mind' ............................... 78
7.2 Techniques for Inducing the Alpha State ............................... 81
7.3 Benefits and Applications of the Alpha State in Daily Life ...... 85

## CHAPTER 8 ............................................................................................. 91

### ENHANCING LEARNING, MEMORY, AND PROBLEM-SOLVING .................. 91
8.1 Techniques for Improving Memory and Learning Capabilities 93
8.2 Applying the Silva Method in Problem-Solving ..................... 96
8.3 Success Stories and Practical Applications ............................ 99

## CHAPTER 10 ......................................................................................... 102

### MENTAL AND PHYSICAL HEALTH ......................................................... 102
10.1 The Mind-Body Connection .............................................. 103
10.2 Using The Silva Method for Mental and Physical Health ..... 106
10.3 Case Studies of Health Improvements with The Silva Method ................................................................................................ 109

## CHAPTER 11 ......................................................................................... 112

### MANIFESTATION AND THE LAW OF ATTRACTION ................................. 112
11.1 The Concept of Manifestation and the Law of Attraction .... 113
11.2 Techniques to Manifest Desires and Attract Abundance ..... 117
11.3 Real Life Success Stories and Applications ......................... 121

## CHAPTER 12 ......................................................................................... 125

### ADVANCED SILVA METHOD TECHNIQUES ............................................ 125
12.1 Accessing the Collective Consciousness ............................ 125
12.2 The Power of Mind Control ............................................... 128

12.3 Implementing Silva Method in Everyday Life..........................131
12.4 The Way Forward: Taking Control of Your Mind's Power...134

## CHAPTER 13 ................................................................................ 137

### THE LEGACY OF JOSÉ SILVA AND THE SILVA METHOD-BASIC INTRO......137
13.1. The global impact of the Silva Method................................139
13.2. Silva Method Today: Silva International.............................141
13.3. Continuing Silva's vision......................................................144

## CHAPTER 14 ................................................................................ 147

### THE FUTURE OF THE SILVA METHOD ........................................................147
14.1. Modern Adaptations and Advancements...........................147
14.2 Predictions and Hopes for the Future ..................................149
14.3. How You Can Be Part of the Silva Method Future...............151

## CONCLUSION ............................................................................. 155

## REFERENCES .............................................................................. 158

# Introduction

Imagine, if you will, that you are trapped in a glass box. The world around you is teeming with life, vibrant and alluring, but you are confined within a small, transparent space. You see the world, you hear the world, you even touch the edges of the world through the glass walls, but you are not a part of it. It feels like you are a spectator rather than a participant. A frustrating experience, isn't it?

For many of us, this glass box is a metaphorical representation of our mental state. We possess a mind so powerful that it can conceive realities beyond ordinary comprehension, yet we often feel confined within its limitations. We dream, we aspire, we desire, but when it comes to realizing our dreams, aspirations, and desires, we hit an invisible barrier.

Studies show that humans use only about 10% of their brain's potential. But what about the remaining 90%? Is it just an evolutionary relic, or is it a vast, untapped reservoir of potential that we have yet to access and harness? If it's the latter, how can we tap into it? These questions have intrigued scientists, philosophers, and curious minds throughout history.

Welcome, dear reader, to "A Workbook to Open Your Mind Using Jose Silva's Method: Achieve Your Mental Freedom Using Simple Exercises From the Most Powerful Book Ever Written for the Human Brain". This book promises a journey of exploration into the depths of your mind, a journey that will liberate you from your self-imposed mental limitations, a journey that will empower you to take control of your mental capacities and wield them with prowess.

In this book, we will explore the groundbreaking method pioneered by Jose Silva, a man who dedicated his life to understanding the mind and unlocking its true potential. A method that has empowered millions across the world, transcending boundaries of culture, geography, and personal backgrounds. We will journey together into the Silva Method, understanding its principles, practicing its techniques, and experiencing its transformative power.

We will uncover the vast potential that lies dormant within us, and we will learn to access and harness it. We will learn to trust our intuition, to use our mind for healing, to improve our memory and learning abilities, and to achieve our personal and professional goals. The path ahead is exciting, challenging, and profoundly rewarding.

We are on the brink of a new era, an era where our understanding of the mind will revolutionize how we live, learn, work, and relate to each other. Recent research indicates that the human brain has the capacity to change and adapt in ways we never thought possible. This concept, known as neuroplasticity, is just one example of the incredible power within us waiting to be harnessed.

Are you feeling stuck in your life, ensnared by the same patterns, the same challenges, over and over again? Are you struggling to break free, to make lasting change, to achieve your heart's deepest desires? Is stress and anxiety a constant companion, robbing you of joy and fulfillment? If these questions resonate with you, know that you are not alone. We all struggle with these challenges. We all long for change, for growth, for liberation from the shackles of our mind's limitations.

In this illuminating book, you will learn the principles and techniques of the Silva Method, a scientifically validated and globally acclaimed approach to harnessing your mind's true potential. You'll discover how to enter the alpha and theta levels of mind consciously and use your newfound mental abilities to shape your reality. You'll learn to heighten your intuition, to heal your body and mind, to improve your memory and learning capabilities, and to set and achieve your personal and professional goals.

Reading this book will transform not only your understanding of your mind but also your life. It will empower you to overcome your mental barriers, to make decisions with clarity and confidence, to live with a sense of peace and joy, and to create the life you've always wanted. It will equip you with tools and techniques you can use throughout your life, tools that will help you navigate the challenges and opportunities that life throws your way.

But why should you choose this book? Because it speaks directly to you, the reader. It understands your struggles, it acknowledges your pain, and it offers a solution that is not only effective but also simple and practical. It provides an opportunity to break free from the chains of limitation and step into a life of freedom and fulfillment.

Now is the time to take the first step towards your mental freedom. Begin your journey now, step into your power, and discover what you are truly capable of. The key to unlocking your mind's potential is within your grasp. All you have to do is turn the page. Let's begin this incredible journey together.

# Chapter 1

## Introduction to The Silva Method

"Whatever the mind of man can conceive and believe, it can achieve." - Napoleon Hill

In a world filled with noise, obligations, and an ever-present sense of time ticking away, the concept of mental freedom might seem elusive, almost impossible. But what if there was a technique that could help you attain that elusive state, a method that could guide you to tap into your mind's unexplored power and lead you towards the path of self-improvement and personal development?

Meet the Silva Method, a scientifically backed mental training program that promises to enhance your intuitive abilities, improve memory, increase creativity, and accelerate your journey towards achieving your life's goals. Named after its founder, Jose Silva, the Silva Method is not just another self-help program—it's a catalyst for transformation.

Jose Silva, a self-educated man with a passion for understanding the mind's capabilities, spent decades researching and developing this unique program. His pursuit of exploring the human mind's uncharted territories stemmed from an innate curiosity to find answers. Over time, this curiosity morphed into a life mission—to empower individuals to utilize their brains more effectively, thereby transforming their lives.

Silva's groundbreaking work has touched millions across the globe, propelling them towards personal growth and development. The Silva Method is about understanding your mind—how it works, and more importantly, how you can make it work for you. It's about accessing a part of your brain that most don't even realize they can reach.

At its core, the Silva Method is a journey of self-discovery. It's a path that takes you into the depths of your mind, uncovering layers of potential you may not have known existed. It's not about changing who you are—it's about becoming the best version of yourself by unlocking your mind's full potential.

It might sound like a tall order. After all, can one method truly provide so many benefits? This is what we aim to explore throughout this book. We invite you to journey with us, exploring your mind's uncharted territories, and uncovering the power that resides within you. Through understanding and applying the Silva Method, you might just discover that the impossible becomes possible, and the elusive becomes attainable.

## 1.1 History and Development of The Silva Method by Jose Silva

The story of the Silva Method began in the small Texas border town of Laredo, in the early 1940s. The man behind it was Jose Silva, an electronics repairman by trade, but a lifelong learner and an explorer of the human mind by passion.

Jose Silva's journey into the world of the human mind was not driven by a conventional academic pursuit. Instead, it was born out of necessity and curiosity. Silva grew up in poverty and had to drop out of school after the 3rd grade to support his family. Despite his limited formal education, he was an insatiable learner, particularly drawn to the workings of the human mind. He taught himself electronics through correspondence courses, and soon he started his own radio repair business.

While working on radios and studying frequencies, he noticed that our minds, much like radios, operated on frequencies too. This realization led him to a more profound question: Could human minds be tuned to operate at optimal frequencies for superior functionality, much like radio devices?

To find an answer, Silva began studying psychology, hypnosis, and parapsychology. Fascinated by his findings, he embarked on a quest to develop a system that could help individuals optimize their mind's functioning. He initially experimented with hypnosis but soon found it limiting because it often led to dependency on the hypnotist.

In search of a better approach, Silva focused his attention on the study of the Alpha and Theta brainwave frequencies, typically associated with deep relaxation, creativity, and intuition. He theorized that if individuals could learn to consciously access these brainwave states, they could harness their full mental potential.

After a decade of rigorous research and countless trial and error, Silva developed a series of mental exercises that enabled individuals to enter the Alpha state at will. He initially tested these exercises on his children, and the results were astounding. Not only did their school grades improve dramatically, but they also displayed heightened intuitive and creative abilities.

Encouraged by these findings, Silva wanted to share his techniques with the world. However, he faced significant resistance from those who dismissed his method as unscientific. But Silva was not deterred. He knew the potential of his work and believed in the power of the human mind.

In 1966, after decades of painstaking research and development, Silva introduced the Silva Method to the public.

The method initially focused on developing psychic abilities. However, as the technique evolved, its scope expanded to cover personal development and self-improvement. It included techniques for stress management, improving memory and learning, increasing creativity, and achieving personal goals.

Silva's hard work and commitment to his method began to pay off when numerous testimonials emerged from those who benefited from it. His method garnered international recognition, and Silva became a well-respected figure in the world of self-improvement and personal development. The Silva Method spread across continents, transforming lives along the way.

Jose Silva passed away in 1999, but his legacy lives on. The Silva Method continues to be a vital tool for those seeking to unlock their mental potential. The Silva Method is not just a testament to the power of the human mind; it is also a tribute to a man who dared to dream, a man who believed in the limitless potential of the human mind. It's a reminder that sometimes, the power to transform our lives lies within us—we just need the right tool to access it.

## 1.2 Overview of The Silva Method: Potential and Goals

"The potential of the average person is like a huge ocean unsailed, a new continent unexplored, a world of possibilities waiting to be released and channeled toward some great good." These inspiring words were spoken by Brian Tracy, a notable self-development author. Tracy's sentiment aligns perfectly with the principles and aspirations of the Silva Method.

The Silva Method is fundamentally a system of practical techniques, designed to guide individuals into a state of relaxed and focused awareness, often referred to as the 'Alpha State'. It's in this state where the magic of the Silva Method truly unfolds.

But what does this mean for you? Well, the promise of the Silva Method is twofold. First, it provides a blueprint to access the reservoir of untapped potential nestled within the contours of your mind. Second, it hands you the steering wheel, allowing you to navigate the course of your life with renewed self-awareness and purpose.

The Potential

When we refer to 'potential', we're speaking about the latent capabilities and resources within us. The Silva Method proposes that we all possess an immense mental potential, much of which remains untapped due to our lack of understanding or inability to access it. This potential includes enhanced learning capabilities, improved memory, increased creativity, heightened intuition, and the ability to manifest our desires.

When you learn to operate in the Alpha State consciously, you tap into these vast, often dormant resources. It's like flicking on a light switch in a previously darkened room, revealing treasures that were always there, merely hidden from view. This potential is what Jose Silva sought to access and harness, not just for himself, but for anyone who was willing to learn.

The Goals

If the Silva Method's potential is the ship, the goals are the compass. They represent the desired destination, the reason why one might want to explore the terrain of their mind.

The goals of the Silva Method are as varied as the people who practice it. However, the overarching objective is to improve the quality of one's life through personal development and self-improvement.

The goals often include but are not limited to:

Achieving Personal Goals: The Silva Method provides techniques to clarify your personal and professional aspirations. It then equips you with the skills to work towards these goals efficiently, using the power of your mind.

Enhancing Creativity and Problem-solving Skills: The Silva Method helps in harnessing your creativity, a powerful tool for innovation and problem solving. When faced with challenges, you're better able to conceive novel solutions.

Increasing Intuition: The Silva Method facilitates the development of intuition. This heightened perception can improve decision-making skills and help steer you towards fulfilling experiences.

Improving Health and Well-being: Stress management is a key component of the Silva Method. The techniques taught help promote relaxation, reduce stress, and ultimately contribute to better physical and mental health.

Manifesting Desires: The Silva Method promotes the ability to manifest desires. It's about aligning your thoughts, emotions, and actions to attract what you want in life.

The potential of the Silva Method paints a picture of a powerful mind, and the goals provide a reason to harness this power. Together, they form a roadmap for anyone seeking to take the journey of self-discovery, self-improvement, and self-mastery. The beauty of the Silva Method lies in its simplicity and practicality. It's not about complex theories or convoluted practices. It's about effective, straightforward techniques that allow you to tap into your mind's potential and align it with your life goals. The journey may be challenging at times, but the rewards are profound. The destination is a life lived consciously, with purpose, fulfillment, and a sense of unlimited possibility.

## 1.3 The Untapped Power of the Mind and How to Access It

"Whatever the mind can conceive and believe, the mind can achieve," said Napoleon Hill, an American self-help author. This quote encapsulates the essence of this section. We'll venture into the expanse of the untapped power of the human mind, and more importantly, provide you with tangible ways to access it.

The human mind is akin to an iceberg, its entirety not immediately visible on the surface. What we are commonly conscious of, our daily thoughts, experiences, and knowledge—these constitute the tip of the iceberg, called the conscious mind. But beneath this, submerged and elusive, is an enormous expanse of untapped potential—the subconscious mind.

So, let's start at the beginning. What exactly is this power that we're referring to? This untapped power of the mind, primarily residing in our subconscious, consists of capabilities such as advanced learning skills, heightened intuition, increased creativity, enhanced memory, and the ability to influence physical and emotional well-being.

Think about it. How often do you catch yourself operating on autopilot, completing routine tasks without any conscious thought? That's your subconscious mind at work. It's an unwavering and diligent worker, performing tasks and storing information without your conscious awareness. But with the right approach, you can make this part of your mind an active ally, learning to tap into its resources for your benefit.

Now that we understand the untapped power within us, the critical question remains: How do we access it?

It's in the response to this question that the Silva Method shines. It offers a systematic approach, a well-marked trail leading to the heart of your mind. Let's break it down into manageable steps.

Step 1: Understanding the States of Mind

Our brain operates in different frequency states, each corresponding to a different level of consciousness. The most familiar states are Beta (alert/waking state), Alpha (relaxed state), Theta (light sleep/ deep relaxation), and Delta (deep sleep). The Silva Method encourages the cultivation of the Alpha state—a deeply relaxed state that serves as a bridge between the conscious and the subconscious mind. It's at Alpha where the mind is most receptive and open, making it the ideal state for harnessing our inherent mental power.

Step 2: Reaching the Alpha State

The Silva Method provides a collection of practical techniques to help you enter and maintain the Alpha state at will. Techniques such as progressive relaxation, visualization, and meditation aid this process. For instance, a simple exercise might involve closing your eyes, taking deep breaths, and imagining a peaceful place. The goal is to slow your brain waves from the Beta to the Alpha state, which fosters an increased connection with your subconscious mind.

Step 3: Programming the Mind

Once you've learned to reach the Alpha state, the next step is learning to use this state effectively. The Silva Method teaches you to program your mind to work towards your goals. It involves techniques like visualization and positive affirmations that help shape your subconscious beliefs and patterns, aligning them with your conscious desires.

For example, if you want to improve your memory, you could visualize yourself remembering information effortlessly and affirm statements like, "I have an excellent memory." When repeated in the Alpha state, these techniques can influence your subconscious mind, leading to improved memory.

Step 4: Harnessing the Power

The final step is learning to harness your mind's power in everyday life. It could be by using it to enhance creativity, make better decisions, improve problem-solving skills, or manifest your desires. The Silva Method offers numerous exercises for this purpose. Regular practice is key here. The more you practice, the more natural it becomes to access and use this power.

The journey to unleashing the untapped power of your mind is undeniably a thrilling one. It's like discovering a hidden treasure within yourself, a reserve of potential just waiting to be unlocked. The Silva Method serves as the key to this treasure, offering a clear and effective roadmap to tap into your subconscious and transform your life in ways you may have only dreamed of.

Remember, this journey isn't a sprint—it's more akin to a marathon. It's about steady, consistent progress rather than immediate, dramatic results. But with patience, persistence, and the right guidance from the Silva Method, you can make your way towards a life of greater mental freedom and unlimited potential.

# Chapter 2

## Understanding Your Mind: Conscious and Subconscious

Have you ever stopped to marvel at the extraordinary capabilities of your mind? It is a powerhouse, a driving force behind everything you do. Our minds shape our thoughts, behaviors, emotions, and in turn, our life stories. But the mind isn't just a singular entity; it's split into two main parts: the conscious and the subconscious. To truly unlock your full mental potential and harness the power of the Silva Method, you must first understand the distinction between these two and how they work in harmony.

The conscious mind is like the captain of a ship, responsible for logical thinking, decision-making, and moment-to-moment awareness. It's the part of your mind that you're using right now as you read these words, as you actively digest this information and make sense of it.

Meanwhile, the subconscious mind is more like the ship itself, powerful and carrying precious cargo. It's a vast storehouse of your memories, experiences, and ingrained beliefs. Operating behind the scenes, it influences your habits, emotions, and instinctual reactions, often without your conscious awareness.

Understanding these two aspects of your mind isn't just intriguing; it's also instrumental for personal growth. When you appreciate how your conscious and subconscious minds interact, you become capable of changing negative patterns, enhancing your intuition, and manifesting your desires. This chapter will guide you on a journey into the heart of your mental machinery, shedding light on the conscious and subconscious minds and showing you how to tap into their combined power. Prepare to discover the immense potential lying within your mind and learn how to steer your own ship towards success, fulfillment, and mental freedom.

## 2.1 Defining Conscious and Subconscious Minds

It's time to get a bit more specific about the nature of our minds. This understanding forms the foundation upon which we can start building our exploration of the Silva Method. Let's start with defining the two key players in our mental theatre - the conscious and subconscious minds.

The Conscious Mind

Think of your conscious mind as the part of your iceberg that is visible above the water. It's the mind you actively engage while you're awake. This mind takes care of all your daily activities, decision-making, and problem-solving needs.

Active Engagement: The conscious mind is fully involved when you're doing things like driving a car, having a conversation, or playing a game. It's at the helm when you're learning something new and need to pay close attention.

Logical Reasoning: The conscious mind is the seat of all logical reasoning. It analyses, compares, and judges every piece of information it encounters. It's the part of your mind you engage when you're solving a crossword puzzle or deciding which pair of shoes to buy.

Short-term Memory: Your conscious mind is also where your short-term memory resides. It keeps track of all the tasks that you need to accomplish in the immediate future.

Decision Making: The conscious mind is responsible for decision-making. It's the part of your mind you use when deciding what to eat for breakfast, how to spend your weekend, or which route to take to work.

The Subconscious Mind

Below the surface, submerged in the depths of your mind, lies the mighty subconscious. It's like the more massive part of the iceberg beneath the water, hidden from view but holding most of the power.

Automatic Functions: The subconscious mind controls all the automatic functions of your body. It keeps your heart beating, your lungs breathing, and your body temperature regulated, without any conscious thought from you. It's tirelessly working in the background, even when you're sleeping.

Long-term Memory: Your subconscious mind is a vast reservoir of long-term memories. It stores experiences from your past that shape your habits, preferences, and personality.

Emotions and Feelings: Your subconscious mind is where your emotions and feelings originate. It's this part of the mind that experiences joy, fear, anger, love, and all other emotions.

Intuition: Your subconscious mind is also the source of intuition or gut feeling. It's capable of processing information from the surroundings on a level that the conscious mind might not immediately understand.

Habits: The subconscious mind is the seat of all your habits. Whether it's a positive habit like regular exercise or a negative one like smoking, it originates and gets cemented here.

Understanding these functions is a significant first step in utilizing your mind to its fullest. The conscious and subconscious minds aren't independent entities, but part of a seamless continuum. They have distinct functions but need to work in harmony for optimal mental and emotional health. In the next section, we will explore the intricate dance between these two aspects of the mind and how their interplay influences our lives. By recognizing their roles and learning how to balance their inputs, we open the door to mental freedom and personal growth. The power of the Silva Method lies in its ability to help us tap into the vast potential of both these minds, enabling us to become the master sculptors of our lives.

## 2.2 The Interaction Between the Conscious and Subconscious Minds

The conscious and subconscious minds, though distinct, don't operate in isolation. They're like two sides of the same coin, each influencing the other in profound ways. The dynamism of their interaction can greatly affect our thoughts, emotions, actions, and overall well-being. To comprehend this interaction, let's first envision a metaphor: Imagine the conscious and subconscious minds as two gardeners tending to the garden of your life.

The Conscious Mind: The Daytime Gardener

The conscious mind can be thought of as the daytime gardener. It's active, alert, and fully engaged during the day, making decisions about what seeds to plant and where. It reads the labels, considers the type of plant, the needed care, and makes deliberate choices about what it wants to see grow in the garden.

Decision-making and Planning: The conscious mind is like the gardener who decides what to plant. It uses logic and reason to make decisions and plan ahead.

Problem-solving: Like a gardener solving problems, such as pest invasions or inadequate sunlight, the conscious mind uses critical thinking to overcome challenges.

Execution of Tasks: The conscious mind puts the plan into action, much like a gardener planting seeds, watering them, and pulling out weeds.

The Subconscious Mind: The Nighttime Gardener

On the other hand, the subconscious mind is like the nighttime gardener. It works in the background, unseen, nurturing the seeds planted during the day. This gardener doesn't question what has been planted; it simply nurtures everything. It doesn't discriminate between the seeds of beautiful flowers and those of invasive weeds; it nurtures them all.

Processing and Internalizing: Just as the nighttime gardener nurtures all seeds, the subconscious mind absorbs and internalizes all thoughts and experiences, positive or negative.

Emotion and Intuition: Much like the nighttime gardener senses the needs of the garden in ways the daytime gardener might not, the subconscious mind is the seat of emotions and intuition.

Maintaining Habits: The subconscious mind maintains habits, both good and bad, just like the nighttime gardener keeps the garden growing, regardless of what has been planted.

The Interplay and Its Impact

The interaction between these two gardeners, or the conscious and subconscious minds, determines the state of your garden, or your life. If the daytime gardener plants seeds of positive thoughts, ambition, and determination, and the nighttime gardener nurtures them well, the result is a flourishing garden representing a life of accomplishment and happiness.

However, if the daytime gardener unknowingly plants seeds of negative thoughts, fear, and doubt, the nighttime gardener will nurture these too. The outcome? A garden overrun with weeds, symbolizing a life clouded by negativity and unfulfillment.

In other words, the thoughts and beliefs you consciously entertain get internalized by your subconscious mind, which then works tirelessly to make them your reality. This interplay is why it's crucial to consciously cultivate positive thoughts, beliefs, and attitudes. It helps ensure that your subconscious mind works on manifesting positivity in your life.

The power of the Silva Method lies in its ability to guide the conscious mind towards positive, goal-oriented thinking and to train the subconscious mind to support this positive direction. By understanding and applying this, you can bring your conscious and subconscious minds into alignment, working together towards your desired outcomes. In the next part of this chapter, we'll discuss how to harness the full potential of both your conscious and subconscious minds, empowering you to cultivate a garden - a life - filled with the flowers of success, happiness, and fulfillment.

A Case Study: Lisa's Story

To help elucidate the interaction between the conscious and subconscious minds, let's consider a real-life example. We'll examine Lisa, a middle-aged woman stuck in a career she didn't enjoy.

Every day, Lisa would consciously tell herself that she disliked her job and yearned for something more fulfilling.

She would ponder on her dissatisfaction, a clear indicator that her conscious mind was "planting" seeds of unhappiness and dissatisfaction in her subconscious mind. However, she wasn't aware of how deeply these thoughts were rooting into her subconscious, which worked quietly in the background, nourishing these seeds without discrimination.

As time passed, Lisa found herself increasingly unhappy and unsatisfied, not just at work but also in her personal life. It was as if a shadow of discontent hung over her every moment. What Lisa didn't realize was that her subconscious mind was merely acting on the seeds sown by her conscious mind. Her consistent thoughts of dissatisfaction had paved the way for her subconscious mind to perceive and promote more of the same feelings, like a garden overrun with the weeds of discontentment.

After a particularly challenging day at work, Lisa stumbled upon a copy of the Silva Method book in a local bookstore. Intrigued, she bought it, not knowing that it was about to change her life.

As Lisa worked through the book, she understood the significance of the interplay between her conscious and subconscious minds. She realized how her conscious thoughts had been feeding her subconscious mind with negativity, which was in turn manifesting in her life.

Inspired to make a change, Lisa began consciously planting more positive seeds. She focused on thoughts of finding a job she loved, picturing herself happy and fulfilled. She envisioned what her ideal job would be like, the tasks she would be doing, and how it would make her feel. As these thoughts became more frequent, her subconscious mind began to nurture these seeds, promoting positive feelings of hope and anticipation within her.

As Lisa changed her conscious thoughts, she noticed a shift in her subconscious responses. She found herself drawn to opportunities she would have previously overlooked. She took online courses that were aligned with her interests, networked with people in her desired field, and gradually transitioned into a new career that brought her immense satisfaction.

Lisa's story is a compelling example of how understanding and harnessing the interaction between the conscious and subconscious minds can lead to significant positive changes in life. The conscious mind sets the direction, and the subconscious mind propels us along that path. They are not opposing forces but a collaborative pair, orchestrating the symphony of our lives.

Harnessing this powerful interaction, as Lisa did, is within your reach. In the next section, we will explore practical exercises that will help you to make the most of your conscious and subconscious minds, allowing you to pave the way towards the life you desire. Together, we will plant seeds of positivity and nurture them, building a garden of your life that is filled with the vibrant colors of happiness, fulfillment, and success.

## 2.3 Accessing the Power of the Conscious and Subconscious Minds

Imagine you're standing on a beach, waves lapping at your feet, a vast ocean of possibilities in front of you. Your conscious mind is like the sandy beach, forming the surface-level thoughts and immediate reactions. On the other hand, your subconscious mind is the deep and boundless ocean, holding all your memories, experiences, and deeply embedded beliefs.

To truly experience the beach, you wouldn't just stand on the shore; you'd also wade into the water, feel the waves, and explore the vastness of the sea. Similarly, to live a fulfilling life, we need to tap into both our conscious and subconscious minds, each holding unique abilities and powers. But how can we utilize the full potential of these two aspects of our mind?

The Conscious Mind: The Director of Your Life

Set Clear Goals: Your conscious mind thrives on clarity. Determine what you want from your life in explicit detail, and let your conscious mind focus on these specific goals.

Make Conscious Decisions: Be deliberate in your actions and decisions. Every choice you make shapes your life, so ensure they are consciously aligned with your goals.

Adopt Mindful Practices: Mindfulness can strengthen your conscious mind. Practices like meditation, yoga, or even simple breathing exercises can enhance focus and awareness.

The Subconscious Mind: The Engine Powering Your Journey

Feed it Positive Affirmations: Just as a garden grows from the seeds planted, your subconscious mind blooms from the thoughts and feelings sowed by your conscious mind. Nurture it with positive affirmations and watch your life flourish.

Visualize Your Success: The subconscious mind responds well to imagery. Visualize your goals as if they are already achieved. The more vivid your visualization, the stronger the impact on your subconscious mind.

Employ Repetition: Your subconscious mind learns from repetition. Reiterate your goals and positive affirmations regularly, and your subconscious mind will gradually align itself with these new beliefs.

Harnessing the Symbiosis

A powerful dynamic exists between your conscious and subconscious minds. By synchronizing these two aspects, you can create a potent force for change and growth in your life.

Consider the case of Thomas, a young man passionate about writing. He consciously set a goal to publish a novel, a dream he had cherished since childhood. Every day, he'd consciously choose to spend hours writing, proofreading, and revising his work. Additionally, he adopted mindfulness practices, meditating each morning to enhance his focus and clarity for the day's tasks.

Meanwhile, Thomas also worked on his subconscious mind. Every night before sleep, he'd affirm, "I am a successful novelist." He'd visualize himself holding his published book, signing autographs, and reading excerpts to a captivated audience. Thomas repeated these affirmations and visualizations daily.

Over time, Thomas noticed his writing improve. He began developing captivating characters, engrossing plots, and his words flowed effortlessly. Thomas credited his progress to the harmonious synchronization of his conscious and subconscious minds.

In the next chapter, we will explore exercises from the Silva Method that will help you utilize the full potential of both your conscious and subconscious minds. Like Thomas, you, too, can harness this powerful duo to create the life you've always dreamt of. Through this journey, remember that the path to mental freedom begins with understanding and utilizing our minds to their fullest potential.

# Chapter 3

## Igniting Imagination and Visualization

Have you ever caught yourself daydreaming, lost in a world of your creation, only to be jolted back into reality? That is the power of your imagination, the incredible ability of the human mind to create, explore, and experience entire worlds and scenarios. Now, what if we told you that you could use this power to bring about significant positive changes in your life? Intrigued? Welcome to Chapter 3, where we delve into the fascinating realm of imagination and visualization, two fundamental aspects of the Silva Method.

Imagination is more than just an escape into daydreams; it's an instrument of transformation. Your mind can't tell the difference between something you vividly imagine and an actual event. When used intentionally, this remarkable feature of our minds can help us shape our reality. We often underestimate the power of our imagination, but it plays a crucial role in personal development and achieving goals.

Visualization takes this one step further, using the mind's eye to see the desired outcomes, facilitating a connection between thought and action. It's a technique used by many successful people across various fields - from athletes preparing for a big game to executives planning for a crucial presentation. They have discovered what you too will learn in this chapter – the significant impact of consciously visualizing your desired outcome.

In this chapter, we will explore the incredible power of imagination and visualization. You'll learn how to ignite your imagination, stimulate creativity, and consciously utilize visualization techniques to impact your reality positively. Through practical exercises, you will be able to bring your dreams closer to reality, making the invisible visible. So, get ready to harness your innate abilities and step into a world of endless possibilities.

## 3.1 The Power of Imagination and Visualization

Step into a quiet room. Let your mind wander, untamed. See an apple. Observe its bright red color, the way its stem curves slightly to the side. Imagine lifting it, the weight of it in your hand, the smooth, cool skin under your fingertips. Picture bringing it to your lips, the crisp crunch when you take a bite, the sweet, slightly tart flavor filling your mouth.

Interesting, isn't it? You've just experienced a piece of the vast power of your imagination and visualization. Even without a physical apple present, your mind could create the sensations as if it were real. This example might seem simple, almost trivial, but the implications are tremendous. Your mind, armed with imagination and visualization, can create realities that don't exist yet but can manifest with focused effort and intent. This is the core of the Silva Method's philosophy and a tool we will learn to harness in this chapter.

Imagination: Your Creative Powerhouse

Our imagination is an extraordinary tool, an internal sandbox where we can build and shape our ideas, and play with possibilities without any real-world repercussions. It fuels our creativity, fosters innovation, and is a cornerstone of problem-solving. When a child plays with an imaginary friend or a cardboard box becomes a castle, we see imagination at its purest, unfettered by the constraints of 'reality.' As we grow older, this creativity often becomes stifled, constrained by societal norms, rules, and a reality grounded in practicality.

However, as proponents of the Silva Method, we understand that preserving and nurturing this ability is crucial. By allowing your mind to roam freely, you ignite creativity, the spark that can ignite a fire of possibilities. Not only does it provide a fresh perspective on old problems, but it also enhances our ability to adapt to new situations, discover novel ideas, and push beyond the confines of conventional thinking.

Visualization: The Blueprint of Reality

Visualization operates like the mind's construction site. If imagination provides the raw materials, visualization is the architect, building on the plans and creating a blueprint for your future reality. When you visualize, you're creating a mental model of what you desire. You're not just thinking about it; you're experiencing it, complete with the associated emotions and sensory experiences.

This process allows you to create a bridge between your current reality and your desired future, giving your subconscious mind a clear and tangible goal to work towards. Your mind does not distinguish between a vividly visualized experience and a real one. So, when you visualize your desired outcomes in detail, your mind starts working as if those outcomes have already occurred.

Visualization isn't merely wishful thinking. It's a scientifically backed process used by successful people across the world. Athletes use visualization to perfect their performance, picturing each movement and outcome before stepping onto the field. Business leaders visualize success scenarios to prepare for important meetings or to set company goals. Musicians, writers, and artists of all sorts use visualization to create masterpieces, first seeing their creation in their mind's eye before bringing it to life.

Uniting Imagination and Visualization

Imagine trying to navigate a dark room. You stumble, uncertain and directionless, because you can't see where you're going. Now, flip on the light switch. Suddenly, the room illuminates, and you can navigate with ease. Imagination and visualization are like that light switch for your mind. They can illuminate the path to your goals, providing clarity, direction, and the means to bring your aspirations to life.

The power of these tools lies in their synergy. Imagination sparks the idea, visualization gives it form, and together, they act as a compass, guiding your subconscious mind towards the realization of your goals. However, like any tool, they require practice to be used effectively.

In the Silva Method, we learn not just to daydream aimlessly, but to imagine with intention, to visualize with clarity and purpose, and to direct these powers towards constructive ends. As we journey through this chapter, we will learn to recognize, harness, and refine these skills. Through practical exercises and a deeper understanding of how our mind works, we will turn our thoughts into actions, our actions into habits, and our habits into the reality we desire.

So, prepare yourself. In the coming sections, we are about to embark on a journey deep into the realms of your mind. We'll start with practical exercises to ignite your imagination, follow it up with techniques to make visualization a part of your daily life, and then learn how to apply these powerful tools to create the life you've always dreamt of. Because, as Albert Einstein once said, "Imagination is everything. It is the preview of life's coming attractions."

## 3.2 Practical Exercises for Igniting Your Imagination

Let's turn now to the realm of imagination, that wondrous, boundless space in your mind. There, your deepest dreams and highest aspirations can be given life, even if just for a fleeting moment. But how do we keep this vibrant, colorful space from fading into a dull, grey canvas as we grow older and life's many challenges cloud our perspective? This section offers you a series of practical exercises to kindle the embers of your imagination, to fan them into a steady flame that can light your path towards achieving your goals.

Exercise 1: The Empty Room

Find a quiet space, free from distractions. Close your eyes and imagine a spacious room. It's empty, save for a solitary chair in the middle. Picture yourself walking towards it, feeling the cool, smooth floor beneath your bare feet. Sit down on the chair and take a moment to let the emptiness surround you. Now, start to fill this room with your thoughts, your dreams, and your desires.

Maybe you envision a grand piano, its polished surface gleaming in the soft light filtering through the window. Perhaps there's a large painting of a serene landscape on one wall. Maybe there's a cosy reading nook in the corner, complete with a soft armchair and a tall, sturdy bookshelf filled with your favorite books. Take your time to fill up the room, giving life to your desires.

This exercise doesn't merely tap into your creativity, it trains your mind to form vivid, detailed mental pictures, an essential skill in the Silva Method.

Exercise 2: Story Builder

Grab a pen and paper, or open a new document on your computer. Write down a single sentence; it could be anything - the start of a story, an observation, a question. Now, build a story around it. As the narrative unfolds, encourage your mind to conjure images, sounds, smells, tastes, and sensations. Try to see the story happening in your mind's eye, like a movie. Feel the emotions of the characters, immerse yourself in the environment, lose yourself in the narrative.

Through this exercise, you're not only stimulating your imagination but also practicing visualization. You're creating a world within your mind, populating it with characters, incidents, and emotions, all of which stem from your imagination. The more vividly you can picture your story, the better.

Exercise 3: The What-If Game

This is a simple but effective exercise that you can do at any time. Simply ask yourself, "What if?"

What if you had the ability to fly?

What if you could breathe underwater?

What if you had the opportunity to meet anyone, alive or dead?

These questions may seem fanciful, but they serve a critical purpose. They push your mind out of its comfort zone, out of the realm of the known and expected, and into a universe of endless possibilities. In this expanded mental space, you'll often stumble upon ideas and insights that you wouldn't have considered otherwise.

Exercise 4: Doodle Your Dreams

For this exercise, all you need is a blank piece of paper and a pen. Set a timer for ten minutes and start doodling. Draw whatever comes to your mind, no matter how random or nonsensical.

This is not about creating a work of art. It's about letting your mind roam freely, letting it express itself without the constraints of logic or judgement.

At the end of the ten minutes, look at your doodles. You might be surprised by what your subconscious mind has expressed through your doodles. This practice helps unlock your creativity and gives you a new avenue to explore your imagination.

Exercise 5: The Future Self

Close your eyes and imagine meeting your future self, ten years from now. Observe how they look, what they're wearing, how they're living, what they've achieved.

This exercise is a powerful way to identify and visualize your goals. You're not merely fantasizing; you're using your imagination as a tool to pave your path to success. The more details you can picture, the more real it becomes in your mind, and the more motivated you'll be to work towards it.

These exercises might seem simple, but their effects are far-reaching. By consistently practicing them, you're not only enhancing your imagination but also honing your visualization skills. Both of these are critical for successfully implementing the Silva Method in your life. So, take your time with these exercises. Practice them regularly and watch as your mind opens up to the endless possibilities it can create.

## 3.3 Applying Visualization Techniques in Daily Life

Having journeyed through the scenic routes of our imagination, it's time now to look at the practical applications of visualization in our day-to-day lives. Visualization isn't merely an abstract concept; it's a tangible skill that, when utilized effectively, can have a substantial impact on your life.

Everyday Applications

Let's begin with a simple example. Suppose you have a job interview scheduled for next week. The thought alone might stir feelings of anxiety. However, if you employ visualization techniques, the scenario changes dramatically.

Picture yourself in the interview room. Visualize the interviewer sitting across from you, friendly and attentive. Feel the confidence coursing through your veins as you answer each question, your voice steady, your demeanor calm. Visualize the interviewer nodding in approval, their face lighting up with impressed recognition.

What you're doing here is mental rehearsal - one of the most common and effective applications of visualization. Athletes have been known to use this technique to enhance their performance. By visualizing their actions, they train their brain to react in a certain way, improving their physical responses in real-life situations.

## Goal Setting

Visualization is a powerful tool in goal setting. It provides a clear vision of your objective, making it feel real and attainable. Let's say you're aiming to start your own business. You could create a vision board, a visual representation of your goal filled with images, quotes, and anything that resonates with your aspiration. Every time you look at it, you remind your mind of your goal, imprinting it deeper into your subconscious. This consistent reinforcement strengthens your belief and motivates you to take action towards achieving your goal.

## Stress Management

Stress is an inevitable part of modern life, but its impact can be significantly reduced through visualization. For instance, when you feel overwhelmed, try to picture a calm, peaceful place - a beach, a forest, a garden. Visualize yourself there, soaking in the tranquility, feeling the stress melt away. This 'mental escape' provides your mind with a much-needed respite, helping you manage stress more effectively.

## Improving Relationships

Visualizing positive interactions can enhance your relationships. Imagine having a fulfilling conversation with a friend or family member. Feel the connection, the understanding, the love. This primes your mind to be more open, compassionate, and communicative, improving your interpersonal interactions.

Enhancing Self-Esteem

Imagine standing in front of a mirror, looking at your reflection with genuine appreciation and self-love. This simple act of visualizing self-acceptance can boost your self-esteem and confidence, affecting all areas of your life positively.

As you incorporate these techniques into your daily routine, you'll find that visualization is not a distant, esoteric concept. It's a practical skill, one that can transform your life in ways you've only dreamed of.

The best part is, there's no 'right' or 'wrong' way to do it. The images, sensations, and emotions that you experience during visualization are personal to you. They stem from your thoughts, your experiences, your desires. So, as you navigate the vibrant landscape of your mind, remember to let your intuition guide you. Your journey is your own, and your destination is but a thought away.

Remember, consistent practice is key when it comes to mastering visualization. The more you exercise this skill, the better you'll become at conjuring vivid, detailed mental images and the more profoundly you'll feel their effects in your life.

So, here's to you, the architect of your dreams. May the power of visualization light your way as you venture into the vast expanse of your mind, paving your path towards the life you've always envisioned.

# Chapter 4

## Core Principles of The Silva Method

The Silva Method, developed by Jose Silva, is not just a program or a course but a movement—a shift in the way we perceive and interact with the world around us. The techniques and principles encapsulated within this method are much more than tools for the improvement of one's mind. They embody a philosophy, a way of life that can change your perspective on what you can achieve and who you can become.

This chapter is designed to give you a clear understanding of the core principles that form the foundation of the Silva Method. It will not just explain what these principles are, but it will also shed light on why they matter, how they work, and how you can apply them to your own life. As we walk through each principle, we aim to make these complex concepts simple and accessible, ensuring that every reader, regardless of their background or experience, can grasp and utilize them.

In addition, we will provide real-life case studies of individuals who have successfully used the Silva Method. Their experiences will provide tangible, concrete examples of how these principles can be put into practice and the kind of transformation they can bring about.

The core principles of the Silva Method are the heart of this system, the driving force behind its success. By understanding and internalizing these principles, you will be taking a significant step towards unlocking your mind's potential and achieving mental freedom. So, let's begin this enlightening journey into the core of the Silva Method.

## 4.1 Foundational Principles of The Silva Method

Every journey begins with a single step, and our exploration into the world of the Silva Method is no exception. The Silva Method is not just a collection of techniques, but it's a transformational philosophy guided by a set of core principles. These principles are the essential pillars supporting the method, the underpinning truths that guide its practice and application.

The first principle is the understanding and acceptance that you possess untapped mental potential. Many people navigate their lives under the assumption that their mental capabilities are limited and fixed, but the Silva Method works from a different premise. The belief is that our minds are immensely powerful entities, with potential far exceeding what most of us dare to imagine. Accepting this premise doesn't merely mean acknowledging it intellectually but genuinely believing in your own potential for greatness. This shift in belief sets the foundation for the rest of the work you will do using the Silva Method.

The second core principle revolves around the conscious use of imagination and visualization. It is a mental technique that involves creating a vivid, compelling image in your mind of what you wish to accomplish. When coupled with strong emotional engagement, visualization can have a profound impact on your subconscious mind, influencing your thoughts, attitudes, and actions. The Silva Method teaches you how to harness the power of visualization, turning it into a potent tool for personal transformation.

A third principle is the importance of relaxation and meditation for accessing deeper levels of consciousness. The Silva Method is unique in its emphasis on achieving an "alpha state," a state of relaxed alertness that enhances learning, creativity, and intuition. Achieving and operating from this alpha state is a fundamental part of the Silva Method. It facilitates deeper mental connections, allowing you to bypass the analytical mind and tap directly into your subconscious, opening the door to profound personal change.

Closely tied to this is the fourth principle: the mastery over your own mental functioning. The Silva Method posits that you are not just a passive recipient of your mental processes but an active director. Through relaxation, visualization, and other techniques, you can learn to guide your mind, using it as a tool to create the life you want. This is not about control in a forceful sense but about harmonious guidance, aligning your conscious and subconscious mind towards a shared goal.

Lastly, the Silva Method operates on the principle of positivity. It emphasizes the importance of maintaining a positive outlook and fostering positive thought patterns. Positive thinking is not about ignoring negative aspects of life but about choosing a perspective that empowers you and supports your growth. The method provides strategies for replacing negative thought patterns with positive ones, leading to improved mental and emotional well-being.

These core principles are the guiding lights of the Silva Method. They provide a framework that enables you to unlock the latent power within your mind and channel it towards your goals and dreams. The rest of this chapter will guide you on how to understand and apply these principles, providing a roadmap that you can follow on your journey to mental freedom. As we explore these foundational principles more deeply, you will gain a clearer understanding of their profound implications for your life.

## 4.2 Understanding and Applying These Principles

Now that we've unveiled the core principles of the Silva Method, the next step is learning how to understand and apply these principles in our lives. We don't just want to read about these principles—we want to truly grasp them, internalize them, and make them part of our everyday experiences. We want to transform these principles from mere words on a page into a living reality.

Let's revisit our first principle: the recognition of our untapped mental potential. It's one thing to hear that we possess unexplored mental powers, but it's quite another to genuinely believe it and operate from this new understanding. Changing deep-seated beliefs can be a challenge, but it's a crucial part of the Silva Method. Start by challenging your limiting beliefs about your mental capabilities. Anytime you catch yourself thinking that you can't do something, pause and reframe that thought. Instead of saying, "I can't," say, "I haven't learned how to do this yet."

Next, we have the principle of visualization. Visualization is more than just daydreaming—it's a focused and purposeful exercise that requires active participation. To effectively visualize, you need to create a clear, detailed mental image of what you want. Use all your senses to make the image as vivid as possible. Feel the emotions you would experience if your goal were already achieved. Practice this daily and you'll soon find your thoughts and actions aligning to make your visualizations a reality.

The third principle—the importance of relaxation and achieving the alpha state—is another crucial part of the Silva Method. It's about learning how to quiet the mind, relax the body, and reach a state of heightened mental awareness. Practicing regular meditation is a great way to start mastering this principle. Schedule in a few minutes each day to sit quietly, focusing on your breath and letting go of any tension in your body. With practice, you'll begin to notice your mind becoming quieter and more focused, making it easier to access your subconscious and tap into your mental potential.

The idea of mastering your mental functioning, our fourth principle, may sound intimidating, but it's really about being aware of your thoughts and emotions and learning to guide them in a positive direction. This involves becoming more mindful, paying attention to your thoughts and feelings without judgment. Recognize when negative thoughts arise and make a conscious effort to replace them with positive ones. This principle is about working with your mind, not against it, fostering a harmonious relationship between your conscious and subconscious mind.

Finally, the principle of positivity is key to implementing the Silva Method. Keeping a positive outlook doesn't mean denying problems or difficulties, but it does mean choosing to focus on solutions and opportunities rather than obstacles. Make an effort to notice the good in each day, no matter how small, and you'll begin to attract more positive experiences into your life.

Applying these principles is a gradual process, one that requires patience, practice, and persistence. But as you begin to integrate these principles into your daily life, you'll start to notice subtle shifts. You'll feel more in control of your mind, more optimistic about your capabilities, and more confident in your ability to shape your life according to your desires.

Remember, the Silva Method isn't just about reading and understanding—it's about doing and experiencing. It's about taking these principles and making them part of your life, transforming your understanding of your mind and its vast potential. This isn't a quick fix, but a lifelong journey of growth, discovery, and transformation. It's about unlocking your mental freedom and stepping into a life of greater joy, fulfillment, and success.

So take these principles, apply them, and witness the power of the Silva Method for yourself. As you do, remember that this is your journey. It's not about perfection, but about progress. It's about moving forward, one step at a time, towards a more empowered and fulfilling life. So let's begin this journey together, using the Silva Method to open our minds and unlock our true potential.

## 4.3 Case Studies of Effective Use of The Silva Method

It's one thing to understand the principles of the Silva Method, but it's another thing entirely to see those principles in action. To truly appreciate the transformative potential of the Silva Method, we'll explore a few case studies, illustrating how individuals have effectively used the Method to make remarkable changes in their lives.

Case Study 1: Embracing Inner Potential—Amanda's Story

Amanda, a mother of two, worked in a demanding corporate job that left her feeling stressed and dissatisfied. Having heard about the Silva Method, she decided to give it a try. The first principle she adopted was acknowledging her untapped mental potential.

She replaced negative self-talk with affirmations of her abilities, insisting that she could handle her job and still find time for her family. This shift in mindset empowered her to negotiate a flexible work schedule, leading to better work-life balance. Amanda's story is an excellent illustration of how embracing our mental potential can lead to positive changes in our lives.

Case Study 2: The Power of Visualization—Robert's Journey

Robert was an aspiring athlete with a big dream: to compete in the Olympics. However, a severe injury threatened his dreams. Determined not to give up, Robert turned to the Silva Method. He began practicing visualization, picturing himself healthy and competing at his best.

The visualization practice went beyond mere thinking; he could feel the adrenaline, hear the crowd's cheers, and see himself crossing the finish line. He incorporated this visualization into his daily routine, especially during physical therapy sessions. Against all odds, Robert recovered from his injury faster than expected and achieved his dream of competing in the Olympics. His story demonstrates the remarkable power of visualization when harnessed correctly.

Case Study 3: Relaxation and Mental State—Linda's Transformation

Linda was a high school teacher who struggled with anxiety, which was impacting her performance and overall well-being. Upon discovering the Silva Method, she was intrigued by the idea of achieving an alpha state for better mental function. She started meditating daily, focusing on achieving a relaxed, serene mental state.

Over time, Linda found her anxiety diminishing. She was better able to manage her stress and found teaching more enjoyable and less overwhelming. Not only did her personal life improve, but her professional life did as well—her improved mental state led to more effective teaching and better relationships with her students. Linda's transformation underscores the incredible benefits of achieving a relaxed mind.

Case Study 4: Mastering Mental Functioning—David's Progress

David, a university student, was having difficulty focusing on his studies. He decided to try the Silva Method to improve his mental functioning. He practiced being more aware of his thoughts and redirecting them towards productive tasks whenever he noticed them straying.

After a few weeks, he found his concentration significantly improved. He was not only able to focus better on his studies but also retain information more effectively. David's story exemplifies how becoming more mindful of our mental processes can lead to significant improvements in our daily life.

Case Study 5: The Impact of Positivity—Olivia's Experience

Olivia, a recent retiree, found herself feeling lonely and aimless after leaving her job. To combat these feelings, she adopted the Silva Method, specifically the principle of positivity. She made a conscious effort to look for the good in each day, no matter how small.

This shift towards a more positive mindset had a profound impact on Olivia. She started engaging in more social activities, found new hobbies, and even started a small business. Her story illustrates how a positive mindset can act as a catalyst for significant life changes.

Each of these case studies highlights the power and potential of the Silva Method when applied

# Chapter 5

## The Power of Positive Affirmations

When you stare at your reflection in the mirror, what do you see? More importantly, what do you say to that person gazing back at you? The language we use when talking to ourselves has a powerful impact on our reality. This is where the power of positive affirmations comes into play, a tool that can transform our lives.

In the quest for mental freedom, positive affirmations are akin to the sunlight that nourishes a budding plant. These affirmations can influence our subconscious minds, fostering an environment of optimism, self-confidence, and determination. They serve as our compass, guiding us towards our goals, even through the stormiest of days.

This chapter will take you on a journey through the realm of positive affirmations. You will gain a clear understanding of the role these affirmations play in shaping your reality, and you'll learn effective strategies for harnessing their potential. This chapter will also introduce you to real-life examples of individuals who have used positive affirmations to transform their lives, providing insights into the power of this mental tool.

Let's begin this journey. The journey that will empower you to change your inner dialogue, leading to a change in your reality. Remember, your words have power, especially when those words are directed towards yourself. Let's learn how to wield this power effectively, transforming it into a catalyst for personal growth and mental freedom. So, are you ready to dive into the incredible world of positive affirmations? Let's start.

## 5.1 Understanding the Role of Affirmations in Shaping Reality

The journey of self-improvement is akin to sculpting a masterpiece from raw marble. Just as a sculptor shapes stone into art, affirmations allow us to mold our thoughts, beliefs, and reality. These powerful, positive statements are the chisel in our hands, and our reality is the block of marble ready to be shaped.

Let's take a moment to consider affirmations. In essence, affirmations are positive, targeted assertions designed to help us conquer self-doubt and negativity. They assist us in visualizing and believing in our affirmed truth, fostering positive change in our lives. An affirmation as simple as, "I am growing stronger and healthier every day," repeated with sincere conviction, can bolster a belief in your wellness.

So, how exactly do affirmations shape reality?

1. Affirmations Target the Subconscious Mind

Recall our previous discussion about the subconscious mind, often compared to a fertile field. In this field, our beliefs are seeds planted by the conscious mind's thoughts and words. With every affirmation, such as "I am confident and capable," we sow the seeds of positivity. As these seeds sprout, they develop into positive beliefs which lead to matching actions.

2. Affirmations Foster a Positive Mindset

Life can often resemble a turbulent sea rather than a tranquil lake. During the stormy times, it's easy to slip into a whirlpool of negativity. However, affirmations are our lifebuoy of positivity. Regularly repeating affirmations like "I stay calm and positive, even in difficult times," encourages a resilient mindset that can weather the storm and recognize opportunities in adversity.

3. Affirmations Influence Our Actions

Our beliefs shape our actions. If you continuously affirm, "I embrace challenges with open arms," you're more likely to seek new experiences, seize opportunities, and persist despite setbacks. Conversely, negative beliefs can deter you from these proactive behaviors. Positive affirmations encourage us to adopt beneficial actions and attitudes.

4. Affirmations Attract Positive Circumstances

The saying "birds of a feather flock together" also applies to our thoughts and circumstances. Positive affirmations, such as "I attract success and prosperity," send out a magnetic signal to the universe, drawing experiences in line with these affirmations.

5. Affirmations Enhance Self-Awareness

The regular practice of affirmations can elevate your self-awareness. Repeatedly affirming, "I am mindful of my thoughts and actions," will make you more cognizant of your thought and behavior patterns. This heightened self-awareness is a potent instrument for personal growth and transformation.

In this light, affirmations are more than optimistic phrases. They're a conscious endeavor to influence and shape our reality actively. Just like the sculptor revealing the beauty hidden within a marble block, we use affirmations to unveil our best selves, ready to be recognized and released into our lives.

## 5.2 How to Use Positive Affirmations for Maximum Effect

Affirmations are like keys. They unlock the latent potential within us. But, as with any key, you need to know how to use it to open the right doors. So, how can we use positive affirmations most effectively? Let's explore together.

1. Be Specific

Specificity in affirmations is like using a GPS for your goals. It guides you straight to your destination. Instead of a vague affirmation like, "I want to be successful," specify what success means to you. If success means becoming a published author, your affirmation might be, "My words captivate readers worldwide, and my books are bestsellers."

2. Stay Positive

The language of your affirmations matters. Focus on the positive outcome you desire, not what you're trying to avoid. For instance, instead of saying, "I will not fail my exams," say, "I excel in my exams." The former focuses on failure, while the latter directs your attention to success.

3. Make It Present

Affirmations are more potent when stated in the present tense. It signals your subconscious mind that your desired outcome is unfolding now. So rather than saying, "I will lose weight," say, "I am healthy, fit, and at my ideal weight."

4. Use Emotionally Charged Language

When your affirmations resonate emotionally, they impact your subconscious mind more deeply. If you're working on building self-confidence, instead of saying, "I am confident," say, "I radiate confidence and charm wherever I go."

5. Regular Repetition

Consistent repetition is a crucial aspect of using affirmations effectively. It's like watering a plant. You need to do it regularly for the plant to grow. Make a habit of repeating your affirmations every morning and night. For instance, repeating, "I am a magnet for success," daily, helps establish this belief deep within your subconscious.

6. Visualize

As you affirm your positive statements, envision them taking shape in your reality. For example, if you affirm, "I am calm and focused during my presentation," visualize yourself on stage, confident, engaging, and delivering a captivating presentation.

7. Embody Your Affirmations

Don't just say your affirmations—live them. Act as if your affirmations are already true. If your affirmation is, "I am financially abundant," manage your finances as a wealthy person would. This doesn't mean overspending, but rather taking wise decisions, investing, and valuing money.

## 8. Record and Listen

In our digital age, technology can be a useful ally. Record your affirmations and listen to them during quiet moments. Hearing your own voice affirming, "I am a successful entrepreneur," amplifies the impact.

## 9. Pair Affirmations with Action

Don't rely on affirmations alone. Pair them with action steps toward your goal. If your affirmation is, "I am physically fit and active," incorporate a daily exercise routine into your schedule.

## 10. Be Patient

Remember, change takes time. You're sculpting your mind and reality, so be patient. Keep affirming, "Every day, in every way, I am getting better and better."

In essence, using affirmations effectively is about creating a deep, emotional connection with your positive statements and integrating them into your daily life. It's about transforming these words from mere sentences into powerful catalysts for change. So embrace the power of affirmations and let them guide you on your journey to self-improvement and success.

## 5.3 Case Studies and Success Stories

To truly understand the power of affirmations, it's enlightening to explore real-life stories of individuals who've harnessed their potency. These tales of transformation offer tangible proof of how affirmations can shape reality. So let's dive into these inspiring narratives and derive insights from their journeys.

Case Study 1: Mark's Journey to Financial Freedom

Mark was struggling with a mountain of debt. He was living paycheck to paycheck, unable to see a way out. That's when he discovered affirmations. Every morning and evening, he began repeating, "I am financially free and abundant."

He visualized his debts disappearing, replaced by a growing bank balance. He saw himself living comfortably, paying bills with ease, and even enjoying luxuries. He also paired this affirmation with actions, such as curbing unnecessary expenses and creating a saving plan.

It was a slow process, but with unwavering belief, his situation started to change. Opportunities to earn extra income presented themselves. He found a higher paying job. His mindset about money transformed from scarcity to abundance. Mark is now debt-free, owning his own house, a testament to the power of affirmations.

Success Story 2: Emma's Conquest of Public Speaking Fear

Emma was a brilliant manager with a petrifying fear of public speaking. This fear was stunting her professional growth. Discovering the potential of affirmations, she decided to confront her fear.

She began affirming, "I am an engaging and confident speaker." She visualized herself delivering captivating presentations to a room full of appreciative listeners. Whenever she had to present, she'd repeat her affirmation, visualize success, and embody confidence. It was challenging initially, but she persevered.

Her presentations started improving. Her voice became steadier, her content more compelling, and her demeanor more confident. Today, Emma is not only a successful manager but also an influential speaker in her organization. Her affirmation had become her reality.

Case Study 3: John's Transformation to a Healthy Lifestyle

John was battling unhealthy eating habits and a sedentary lifestyle. A routine health check-up was a wake-up call for him. He decided to leverage affirmations to transform his lifestyle.

His affirmation was, "I am fit, healthy, and enjoy an active lifestyle." He visualized himself enjoying workouts, choosing healthy food, and feeling energized. John also incorporated a balanced diet and a regular exercise routine into his daily schedule.

His cravings for junk food decreased, and he started enjoying his workouts. His health parameters improved dramatically, and he felt more vibrant and active. John's journey is an inspiring testament to how affirmations can drive profound changes in one's lifestyle and health.

Success Story 4: Sarah's Journey to Self-Love

Sarah had always struggled with self-esteem and self-love. She always focused on her flaws and never truly appreciated herself. The discovery of affirmations was a game-changer for her.

Sarah started to use the affirmation, "I love and accept myself exactly as I am." She visualized herself happy, confident, and surrounded by love. It was hard at first because it was the opposite of her habitual thinking. But she persisted.

Gradually, her perception of herself began to shift. She started recognizing her strengths and accepting her weaknesses. She felt more comfortable in her skin and started expressing herself authentically. Today, Sarah radiates self-confidence and self-love, influencing others around her positively.

Each of these individuals embarked on different journeys, facing unique challenges. But they all had a common tool: positive affirmations. Their stories stand as a testament to the transformative power of affirmations, and they serve as motivation for all of us. As we conclude this chapter, let their stories inspire you to craft your own affirmations and start your journey of transformation.

# Chapter 6

## Shaping Your Belief System

"Believe you can and you're halfway there," said Theodore Roosevelt, the 26th President of the United States, and he couldn't have been more right. Your beliefs, often underestimated, serve as the foundation upon which you build your life. This chapter, "Shaping Your Belief System," delves into the significance of your beliefs and how they profoundly influence your experiences.

At the core of our very existence, our belief systems guide our thoughts, shape our behaviors, and, in turn, define the reality we live in. They are the intricate map that leads us through life, influencing our choices, reactions, and even our ability to face and overcome challenges. Like a director behind the scenes, our beliefs quietly write the script of our lives.

But what happens when this director starts scripting our downfall? What happens when negative thought patterns and limiting beliefs sneak into the framework, distorting our perspectives and hampering our potential? It is then that we need to seize the reins and rewrite the script.

This chapter will guide you through understanding the role of your beliefs, identifying detrimental thought patterns, and effectively transforming them. With the Silva Method as our compass, we'll navigate this process, providing practical exercises that will empower you to curate a belief system that uplifts you, propels you towards your goals, and helps shape a fulfilling life.

Remember, reshaping your beliefs is not an overnight endeavor. It requires patience, persistence, and above all, a commitment to self-growth. But rest assured, every step you take on this journey will bring you closer to attaining the mental freedom that the Silva Method promises. Let's commence this enlightening journey together.

## 6.1 How Beliefs Shape Experiences

"A man is but the product of his thoughts. What he thinks, he becomes," said Mahatma Gandhi, one of the most influential figures of the 20th century. Such words hold an essential truth about the profound influence of our beliefs on the experiences we manifest in our lives.

Beliefs are like the glasses through which we view the world. They are fundamental in shaping our perceptions and consequently, our experiences. Just as a pair of sunglasses can change the way we see the colors and contours around us, so can our beliefs alter our perception of reality. Essentially, they determine our approach to life and color our interpretation of events and interactions.

Let's explore this with an example. Consider two individuals, John and Mary. John has a strong belief in his capabilities. He believes that challenges are opportunities for growth. Mary, on the other hand, holds the belief that she is not as capable as others, and perceives challenges as insurmountable obstacles.

When faced with a complex project at work, John, with his positive belief system, tackles it with enthusiasm. He perceives difficulties as learning opportunities, and with each hurdle he overcomes, his self-confidence grows. His belief in his abilities creates a positive feedback loop that fuels his progress, leading him to successfully complete the project.

In contrast, Mary approaches the same project with anxiety and doubt. She views every difficulty as a confirmation of her inadequacy. Instead of fueling progress, her negative belief system fuels a downward spiral of self-doubt and hesitancy, hampering her performance.

While both John and Mary faced the same circumstance, their contrasting beliefs led them to vastly different experiences. This example illustrates how our beliefs can shape our realities, turning them into self-fulfilling prophecies.

Indeed, the impact of our beliefs extends beyond personal experiences and affects our relationships as well.

Imagine holding the belief that people are inherently untrustworthy. With this perspective, you might misinterpret innocent actions as deceitful, leading to misunderstandings and strained relationships. Conversely, if you believe in the inherent goodness of people, you'll likely foster harmonious relationships filled with mutual respect and understanding.

The power of belief can even affect our physical health. For instance, research indicates that individuals who believe in their ability to recover from illness often experience better health outcomes. This phenomenon, known as the placebo effect, demonstrates how our beliefs can influence our physiological responses.

Recognizing how our beliefs shape our experiences is the first step towards harnessing this power for positive change. We cannot control all external events, but we can control our beliefs. By consciously curating a belief system that empowers us, we can significantly improve our experiences, relationships, and overall quality of life.

As we journey further into this chapter, we'll guide you through the process of identifying and transforming detrimental thought patterns. With the Silva Method by our side, we'll strive to reshape our beliefs to ones that lift us towards achieving our goals and fostering a life of fulfillment. It all begins with understanding that our beliefs are more than passive thoughts - they are the architects of our reality.

## 6.2 Identifying Negative Thought Patterns and Limiting Beliefs

As Mark Twain once humorously observed, "I've had a lot of worries in my life, most of which never happened." This jesting remark conceals a potent truth about the human condition: much of our discomfort stems not from external circumstances, but from our own internal thought patterns, often tending towards the negative. Our minds can become entangled in a web of self-deprecating thoughts, fears, and anxieties, even when our external reality offers little cause for such concerns. If these thoughts are unchecked, they can solidify into limiting beliefs that shape our experiences, relationships, and aspirations.

Negative thought patterns, also known as cognitive distortions, distort our perception of reality, instilling in us a sense of helplessness, inadequacy, or unworthiness. To loosen their grip, we must first learn to identify them. In this section, we will explore some common negative thought patterns and discuss how you can recognize them in your daily life.

One common pattern is 'all-or-nothing thinking', also known as 'black and white thinking'. In this mindset, there is no middle ground: you either succeed or fail, you're either perfect or a complete disaster. For example, if you received a critique at work, you might think, "I'm a total failure," rather than seeing it as a chance for growth.

Another pattern is 'overgeneralization'. This happens when you take one negative experience and generalize it to all related situations. Say you tripped over while dancing at a party. An overgeneralization might be, "I'm terrible at dancing, I'll never dance again." This response inhibits your ability to learn and grow from the experience.

'Catastrophizing' is another prevalent pattern. This involves imagining the worst possible outcome in any given situation. For instance, if a loved one doesn't answer your phone call, you might immediately think, "Something terrible has happened," rather than considering less dramatic possibilities, like they simply forgot their phone at home.

While these are just a few examples, negative thought patterns can take many forms. Identifying them requires introspection, honesty, and a little detective work. A good place to start is to observe your thoughts and feelings, especially when you're facing challenging situations. Write them down in a journal and examine them later when you're in a more relaxed state of mind.

Now, let's discuss limiting beliefs. These are deeply held convictions that constrain our potential. They are often formed in childhood, and are usually subconscious, making them harder to detect. They might manifest as thoughts like, "I'm not good enough," "I don't deserve happiness," or "I'll never be successful."

Like negative thought patterns, identifying limiting beliefs involves introspection and honesty. One technique to uncover them is to consider your fears and insecurities, as they often stem from these deep-seated beliefs. Another approach is to notice recurring patterns in your life. If you consistently find yourself facing similar obstacles, there might be a limiting belief at work.

Another way to uncover limiting beliefs is to listen to your inner critic. This voice inside your head often speaks in 'shoulds' and 'shouldn'ts' and uses them to impose self-limitations. Recognize that this voice isn't the ultimate authority on your capabilities and worth, but a manifestation of your limiting beliefs.

Identifying negative thought patterns and limiting beliefs is the first step towards overcoming them. In doing so, we allow ourselves to confront the ghosts that haunt our minds and begin the process of mental liberation. It's akin to cleaning out a cluttered room - at first, the task may seem daunting, but as you sort through each item, making decisions on what to keep and what to discard, the space begins to clear. Similarly, as you sort through your thought patterns and beliefs, deciding which serve you and which don't, your mind begins to clear, making way for positivity and growth.

## 6.3 Techniques for Replacing Negative Thoughts with Positive Ones

Having identified our negative thought patterns and limiting beliefs, the question arises: how can we free ourselves from these burdensome thoughts and replace them with more empowering ones? It's one thing to identify an unwelcome houseguest, but quite another to usher them out and bar the door against their return. Fortunately, the Silva Method offers effective techniques for transforming our mindscape from a stormy sea of negativity into a serene haven of positivity.

The first tool in our arsenal is 'cognitive restructuring', a technique that involves recognizing, challenging, and replacing negative thoughts. Think of it as a mental courtroom where you are both the defendant (the one holding the negative thought) and the attorney (the one challenging the thought). For instance, if you catch yourself thinking, "I'm terrible at public speaking," challenge this belief with evidence to the contrary, such as times when you spoke effectively in a group setting. Over time, these 'courtroom battles' can lead to a significant shift in your thinking.

A second technique is 'affirmations'. Affirmations are positive statements about ourselves and our abilities that, when repeated, can influence our subconscious mind and reinforce our self-belief. They are most effective when stated in the present tense, are personal, and carry a strong emotional charge. An example might be, "I am a confident and compelling speaker." Try to repeat your chosen affirmations daily, ideally first thing in the morning and last thing at night when your mind is in a receptive state.

Another powerful technique is 'visualization', a cornerstone of the Silva Method. Visualization is the process of creating vivid mental images of the outcomes we desire. Our minds often struggle to distinguish between real and imagined events, so by visualizing positive scenarios, we can 'trick' our brains into believing these scenarios are our reality. For instance, if you're anxious about an upcoming presentation, visualize yourself delivering it confidently and successfully, receiving applause from your audience. Feel the excitement, relief, and satisfaction in your body as you immerse yourself in this positive visualization.

'Gratitude practice' is another powerful antidote to negativity. By regularly acknowledging and expressing gratitude for the good things in our lives, we shift our focus from what's wrong to what's right, leading to a more optimistic outlook. Try keeping a 'gratitude journal' and aim to list at least three things you're grateful for each day.

A final, and crucial, technique is 'mindfulness meditation'. This practice involves focusing our attention on the present moment and accepting it without judgment. It encourages us to observe our thoughts and feelings as they arise, without getting caught up in them. This can create a sense of detachment from our negative thoughts, allowing us to recognize them as transient mental events rather than absolute truths. Over time, regular mindfulness practice can lead to a more balanced, positive mental state.

While these techniques can be highly effective, remember that transforming ingrained thought patterns and beliefs is not a quick fix. It's a journey, requiring patience, persistence, and self-compassion. There may be times when you stumble, when old patterns resurface, but that's all part of the process. In those moments, offer yourself compassion, gently remind yourself of the truth of your worth, and continue along the path.

Each step you take, each negative thought you replace with a positive one, is a victory. Over time, these small victories will accumulate, like drops of water forming a mighty ocean, leading to a profound shift in your mental landscape, and in turn, your life. By harnessing the power of the Silva Method, you hold the keys to unlock your mental freedom, and step into your fullest potential. Let's continue this journey together, towards a future brimming with positivity, possibilities, and peace.

# Chapter 7

## Entering the Alpha State of Mind

Welcome to Chapter 7, where we set out on an exciting exploration of the 'Alpha State of Mind'. This topic is a cornerstone of Jose Silva's Method, and rightly so. It's a state of enhanced relaxation and concentration, one where the conscious and subconscious mind can work together harmoniously. By learning to enter the Alpha State at will, we can unlock powerful tools for self-improvement and transformation.

The Alpha State is a unique mental state marked by slower brainwave activity. It's that sweet spot between wakefulness and sleep, a doorway to the subconscious mind. It's often experienced during activities such as meditation, deep relaxation, or just before falling asleep or waking up. The essence of this state is a relaxed alertness, a tranquil concentration that opens the door to intuition, creativity, and heightened learning.

In this chapter, we'll break down the Alpha State concept, providing you with a clear understanding of its nature and significance. We'll guide you through tried-and-tested techniques to help you induce this state at will. Finally, we'll discuss its diverse benefits and practical applications in daily life.

By the end of this chapter, you'll have gained valuable insights into accessing and utilizing the Alpha State of Mind. You'll be equipped with the tools to tap into a reservoir of calm, creativity, and intuition, empowering you to navigate life's challenges with a heightened sense of clarity and control.

So, ready to start this transformative journey? Let's dive in and demystify the intriguing realm of the Alpha State of Mind. It's time to step into an empowering chapter of your self-development journey. Let the adventure begin!

## 7.1 Understanding the 'Alpha State of Mind'

Let's embark on our exploration of the 'Alpha State of Mind.' The concept of the Alpha State is deeply embedded within the universe of mind exploration and control, acting as a bridge that unites the conscious and subconscious aspects of our psyche. But, what exactly is the Alpha State of Mind? And what significance does it hold in our pursuit of mental freedom and self-improvement? Let's illuminate these intriguing questions.

The Science Behind the Alpha State

Before we dive deeper, it's crucial to ground our understanding of the Alpha State in the realm of brainwave science. Our brains constantly emit electrical signals, which can be measured using an electroencephalogram (EEG). The patterns and speed of these signals give rise to different states of consciousness, represented by five primary types of brainwaves: Delta, Theta, Alpha, Beta, and Gamma.

The Alpha State corresponds to the 'alpha' brainwaves that operate at a frequency of approximately 8 to 12 Hz. This state is typically associated with a calm, relaxed alertness. It's that sweet middle ground between the drowsy, dreamlike Theta state and the hyper-alert, focused Beta state. Think of it as the brain's 'neutral gear,' a state of balanced awareness that's neither too drowsy nor too alert.

Characteristics of the Alpha State

The Alpha State is often likened to a state of 'flow,' a harmonious engagement with an activity where you lose track of time and become fully immersed in the present moment. If you've ever found yourself engrossed in a creative task, enjoying a peaceful moment in nature, or lost in a good book, chances are, you've tasted the Alpha State. It's a space where calm meets concentration, relaxation meets awareness, and creativity blossoms.

During this state, your mind remains alert, but your body achieves a deep level of relaxation. It's almost as if the outer world fades away, leaving you in a serene bubble of introspection and focus. The Alpha State allows for increased visualization ability, improved learning, heightened creativity, and a richer connection with your intuitive faculties.

Alpha State: The Gateway to the Subconscious Mind

What sets the Alpha State apart is its role as the gateway to the subconscious mind. As we've discussed in earlier chapters, our subconscious is like the 'control center' of our beliefs, memories, and innate abilities. It's the underlying force that shapes our behaviors, emotions, and decisions, often without our conscious awareness.

The Alpha State allows us to tap into this potent reservoir of subconscious information. It's akin to opening a communication channel with our deeper self, creating a two-way dialogue between our conscious intentions and subconscious patterns. By learning to enter and maintain the Alpha State, we can direct our subconscious towards the change and growth we seek.

Alpha and Meditation

The Alpha State is commonly experienced during meditation and other relaxation practices. In meditation, as you release your attachment to external stimuli and turn inward, your brainwave activity slows down from the active Beta State, entering the peaceful Alpha State. It's within this tranquil realm that we find the clarity and calm that meditation brings.

However, this state is not limited to seasoned meditators. Almost everyone has experienced alpha brainwaves during moments of daydreaming, just before sleep, or upon waking up. These are times when we naturally descend into a more relaxed state of mind, allowing the conscious mind to take a back seat while the subconscious comes to the fore.

In sum, the Alpha State of Mind is a potent tool in our quest for personal transformation. It's the 'sweet spot' of relaxed attentiveness that allows us to access our subconscious capabilities while maintaining conscious control. In the following sections, we'll explore how to tap into this powerful state deliberately and how it can enhance various aspects of our daily lives.

Understanding the Alpha State is the first step towards mastering it. Now that we've laid the groundwork, we're ready to explore practical techniques to induce this state, further strengthening your ability to harness the immense power of your mind.

## 7.2 Techniques for Inducing the Alpha State

Now that we've demystified the Alpha State of Mind, it's time to navigate the practical part of our journey: learning how to access this serene and productive mental zone at will. This chapter will provide you with a variety of techniques to successfully induce the Alpha State, with practical instructions and guidance at each step.

Breath-Focused Meditation

Breath-focused meditation is a simple yet highly effective technique for inducing the Alpha State. By directing our full attention to the breath, we anchor our mind to the present moment, easing the transition from the alert Beta state to the relaxed Alpha state.

Let's explore this technique step-by-step:

Find a quiet place: Choose a tranquil environment where you won't be disturbed. This could be a dedicated meditation space, your bedroom, or even a secluded corner in a park.

Get comfortable: Sit comfortably on a chair or a cushion, keeping your back straight. You could also lie down if that's more comfortable for you.

Close your eyes: Gently close your eyes. This will help minimize external distractions and promote inner focus.

Focus on your breath: Turn your attention to your breathing. Observe the natural rhythm of your breath as it flows in and out. Notice the coolness of the air as you inhale and its warmth as you exhale.

Mindful observation: If your mind wanders, gently bring your focus back to your breath. Don't criticize yourself for any distractions. Remember, the objective is not to eliminate thoughts but to avoid getting entangled in them.

Continue the practice: Maintain this mindful observation for 10-15 minutes or as long as you feel comfortable. With regular practice, you'll find it easier to slip into the Alpha State.

Progressive Muscle Relaxation

Progressive Muscle Relaxation (PMR) is a technique that can help you achieve a deep state of physical relaxation, which often leads to the Alpha State. The process involves tensing and relaxing different muscle groups in your body sequentially.

Here's how you can practice PMR:

Find a comfortable spot: Start by finding a quiet, comfortable place where you won't be disturbed. You can sit or lie down, whichever you prefer.

Starting point: Begin with your toes. Tense them as much as you can without causing discomfort. Hold this tension for about five seconds.

Release: After five seconds, release the tension, letting all the stress flow out of your toes. Notice the contrast between the tensed and relaxed states.

Move upwards: Repeat this process with different muscle groups, moving upward from your toes. Engage your feet, calves, thighs, and continue up to your face.

Complete relaxation: By the time you've tensed and relaxed each muscle group, your entire body should feel deeply relaxed, paving the way for you to slide into the Alpha State.

Guided Visualization

Guided visualization involves using your imagination to create peaceful and calming mental images. These positive scenarios help in shifting your brainwave activity from the Beta state to the Alpha state.

Here's how to go about it:

Choose your visualization: Begin by choosing a scenario that brings you peace. It could be a serene beach, a tranquil forest, or even a moment from your past filled with happiness and calm.

Engage your senses: Close your eyes and visualize this place or scenario. Engage all your senses. What do you see? What sounds can you hear? Can you smell or taste anything?

Embrace the feelings: Let the peace and happiness from this visualization wash over you. Embrace the positive emotions that emerge.

Return gently: After spending some time in this visualization, gently bring yourself back to your current surroundings. Open your eyes slowly, carrying the tranquility of the Alpha state with you.

Each of these techniques offers a unique path to the Alpha State. As you experiment, you'll likely find one method more effective or enjoyable than the others. That's perfectly fine. Stick with what works for you. Remember, the aim is not just to reach the Alpha State, but to do so in a way that feels natural, comfortable, and enriching for you.

## 7.3 Benefits and Applications of the Alpha State in Daily Life

Understanding the Alpha state is just the beginning; truly harnessing its power comes from incorporating it into everyday life. By doing so, we can gain the myriad benefits it offers, spanning from improved mental health to enhanced creativity. Let's explore these benefits in more detail, and discuss how you can apply the Alpha state to different areas of your life.

Improved Mental Health

Alpha brainwaves are linked with reduced levels of stress and anxiety. When you are in the Alpha state, you experience a deep sense of calm and relaxation, which can counteract the harmful effects of stress hormones in the body. By regularly inducing the Alpha state through the techniques we discussed in the previous section, you can cultivate an overall state of mental wellbeing.

For example, if you are feeling particularly anxious before an important meeting, take a few minutes to engage in breath-focused meditation or progressive muscle relaxation. This will help you transition to the Alpha state, thus lowering your anxiety levels and enabling you to approach the situation with a calm and clear mind.

Enhanced Learning and Memory

The Alpha state has also been associated with improved learning abilities and memory recall. While in this state, the mind is calm and receptive, making it an ideal condition for learning new information and skills. This could be particularly useful for students or professionals seeking to expand their knowledge.

Let's say you're trying to learn a new language. Instead of forcing yourself to memorize new vocabulary and grammar rules in a stressed state, try transitioning to the Alpha state first. The calmness and focus associated with the Alpha state can enhance your ability to absorb and retain new information.

Increased Creativity

One of the most fascinating benefits of the Alpha state is its potential to unlock our creative capacities. The relaxed yet alert state of mind can encourage divergent thinking, allowing us to see things from different perspectives and come up with unique solutions.

Consider a time when you're facing a creative block, such as when you're struggling with a design or writing project. By inducing the Alpha state, you may be able to see past the block and discover creative insights that were previously elusive.

Enhanced Physical Health

The benefits of the Alpha state are not limited to mental wellbeing. Regular induction of this brainwave state can lead to significant physical health benefits as well. By reducing stress and promoting deep relaxation, the Alpha state can improve sleep quality, lower blood pressure, and strengthen the immune system.

For instance, if you're having difficulty sleeping, inducing the Alpha state before bedtime can calm your mind and body, preparing you for a night of restful sleep.

These are just a few examples of how the Alpha state can improve your everyday life. However, the potential applications are as diverse as our daily activities and challenges. By learning to induce the Alpha state at will, we gain a powerful tool that can enhance our wellbeing, productivity, and overall quality of life.

Experiencing the Alpha State: A Guided Exercise

Now, let's turn our learning into practice. We'll go through a guided exercise that will help you enter the Alpha state and start enjoying its benefits. Remember, as with any skill, it takes practice to become proficient. Be patient with yourself and keep an open mind.

Step 1: Find a Quiet Place

Start by finding a quiet and comfortable place where you won't be disturbed. This could be your bedroom, a peaceful corner of your garden, or even a secluded spot in a local park. The key is to have an environment that feels safe and tranquil.

Step 2: Get Comfortable

Sit or lie down in a comfortable position. If you're sitting, keep your back straight but relaxed. If you're lying down, ensure your body is aligned and relaxed. Close your eyes to shut out any visual distractions.

Step 3: Deep Breathing

Begin by taking slow, deep breaths. Inhale deeply through your nose, hold your breath for a few seconds, and then exhale slowly through your mouth. Focus on the sensation of your breath entering and leaving your body.

Step 4: Progressive Muscle Relaxation

Next, focus on relaxing each muscle group in your body. Start with your toes, slowly moving up to your feet, your legs, your abdomen, your arms, and finally your face. As you focus on each muscle group, consciously release any tension you feel.

Step 5: Visualization

Now, imagine a calm, serene place. It could be a quiet beach, a peaceful forest, or any place that you associate with relaxation and peace. Imagine yourself in this place, experiencing it with all your senses. This will help shift your brainwave activity towards the Alpha state.

Step 6: Affirmations

In this relaxed state, repeat some positive affirmations. These could be phrases like, "I am calm and relaxed," or "I am in control of my thoughts." This step is optional, but it can enhance the benefits of the Alpha state, particularly in terms of mental wellbeing.

Remember, the goal here is not perfection, but practice. It's okay if your mind wanders or if you don't achieve the Alpha state right away. Be patient and kind to yourself, and remember that with regular practice, entering the Alpha state will become easier and more natural.

Now that we have a practical understanding of inducing the Alpha state, let's proceed to discuss more applications in daily life.

# Chapter 8

# Enhancing Learning, Memory, and Problem-Solving

Welcome to a captivating exploration into the depths of your mind. In this chapter, we will examine the phenomenal powers of learning, memory, and problem-solving. Using Jose Silva's methods, we will venture into the recesses of our intellect, shedding light on the remarkable capabilities lying dormant within us, and learning to harness these tools to improve our lives.

In today's fast-paced world, learning effectively, retaining information and solving problems swiftly have become essential skills. It's not just about passing exams or excelling at work; these skills help us navigate life, enabling us to process new information, adapt to changes, and make informed decisions. However, amid the hustle and bustle, our minds can become clouded, and our ability to learn and remember can be hindered.

Enter Jose Silva's methods - a beacon of hope in this complex maze of mental abilities. Through his techniques, we can enhance our learning and memory capacities, allowing us to absorb information more effectively and recall it with greater precision. With regular practice of these methods, your mind becomes a well-oiled machine, primed for efficient learning and extraordinary recall.

But our mental journey doesn't stop at learning and memory. The same tools that empower these functions can be repurposed for problem-solving. With Silva's methods, we can train our minds to see beyond the obvious, uncovering innovative solutions to challenges we face in our everyday lives. Whether it's a personal issue, a work-related conundrum, or a creative block, our enhanced mind can provide solutions that previously eluded us.

As we progress through this chapter, we'll also explore success stories from individuals who have applied Silva's techniques to enhance their learning, memory, and problem-solving abilities. Through these real-world examples, you will witness the power and potential of Silva's methods, instilling confidence and motivation to apply these techniques in your own life.

Now, let's dive into the intricate workings of our mind and explore the fascinating world of learning, memory, and problem-solving through the lens of Jose Silva's enlightening methods. So gear up and get ready to unlock the hidden treasures of your mind!

## 8.1 Techniques for Improving Memory and Learning Capabilities

Have you ever marveled at the mind's astounding ability to retain information? The human brain, with its capacity to store and recall knowledge, truly is an extraordinary organ. In this section, we'll explore practical techniques drawn from the Silva Method that can help enhance your memory and boost your learning abilities.

Understanding Memory and Learning

Let's start our journey with a simple understanding of memory and learning. At its core, learning is the process of acquiring new information or skills, while memory is the ability to retain and recall that information when needed. These two cognitive functions are closely interlinked. You learn new information, your memory stores it, and when needed, you recall it.

Silva's Techniques for Enhanced Memory

Relaxation and Visualization: Stress can create a significant barrier to effective memory and learning. One of Silva's primary techniques is the use of relaxation and visualization to reduce stress, thereby creating a more conducive environment for memory and learning. Regularly practicing this technique can lead to an improved ability to remember.

Exercise: Find a quiet place, close your eyes, and visualize a calming scene. It could be a serene beach or a tranquil forest. As you immerse yourself in this scene, allow your body and mind to relax. Practice this exercise daily for optimal results.

Association: Silva taught that our brain learns and remembers best when information is associated with something meaningful or familiar. This technique involves linking new information to existing knowledge or experiences, forming strong memory pathways.

Exercise: When learning new information, try to relate it to something you already know or have experienced. For instance, if you're trying to remember a new colleague's name, you might associate it with a celebrity or a character from a favorite book who shares the same name.

Repetition: Silva emphasized the value of repetition in strengthening memory. Repeatedly reviewing information helps consolidate it in our long-term memory, making it easier to recall when needed.

Exercise: Create a schedule for reviewing new information. For example, if you're studying for an exam, review your notes after one day, then after three days, and again after one week.

## Silva's Techniques for Improved Learning

Goal Setting: According to Silva, setting specific goals can enhance learning. This technique encourages you to be clear about what you want to learn, providing a direction to your learning process.

Exercise: When starting to learn something new, write down your learning goals. What do you want to achieve from this learning process? Having a clear aim can make your learning more targeted and effective.

Active Engagement: Silva believed in the power of active engagement in learning. This involves immersing yourself in the learning process, asking questions, discussing ideas, and seeking to apply the knowledge.

Exercise: Don't just passively read or listen to information. Engage with it. Ask questions, participate in discussions, and look for opportunities to apply what you've learned.

Visualization: Just as in improving memory, Silva advocated the use of visualization for learning. By visualizing the application of new knowledge or skills, you can enhance your understanding and retention.

Exercise: After learning something new, close your eyes and visualize yourself using that information or skill. This can help consolidate your learning and make it easier to apply the new knowledge when needed.

While these techniques may appear simple, their consistent application can lead to profound improvements in memory and learning. Remember, the key lies in regular practice. With patience and persistence, you can harness the power of Silva's techniques to unlock the true potential of your memory and learning abilities.

As we move forward, we will explore how these techniques can be applied in problem-solving. We'll also learn about those who have applied Silva's methods in their lives and the remarkable successes they have achieved. So stay tuned and get ready to unlock more hidden treasures of your mind!

## 8.2 Applying the Silva Method in Problem-Solving

Problem-solving is a critical skill that everyone needs in their daily life. Whether it's a complex business problem or a trivial everyday issue, effective problem-solving skills can make our lives significantly easier. This section will guide you on how to leverage the Silva Method in honing your problem-solving abilities.

According to Silva, every problem, regardless of its complexity, can be solved by tapping into our subconscious mind. The subconscious mind, often neglected in traditional problem-solving approaches, holds a wealth of creativity and wisdom that can provide innovative solutions. But how do we tap into this remarkable resource? Silva provides practical techniques to help us do just that.

Relaxation and Intuition: As with improving memory and learning, the first step is relaxation. By calming our conscious mind, we can better access our subconscious and its insights. Additionally, fostering intuition can lead us to answers that might not be immediately apparent.

Exercise: The next time you face a problem, instead of rushing to solve it, take a moment to relax. Close your eyes, take deep breaths, and let your mind calm down. Then, ask your subconscious mind for a solution and let your intuition guide you.

Consider Jane, a manager at a software company. She was grappling with a team conflict issue that was impacting productivity. Rather than jumping into the fray with a directive approach, Jane used this technique. She took a step back, relaxed, and asked her subconscious mind for guidance. To her surprise, the solution she intuitively felt was not to impose more rules, but to facilitate a team-building exercise to enhance understanding and empathy among team members. This intuitive solution not only resolved the conflict but also strengthened the team's cohesion.

Visualization: Visualizing the problem and its potential solutions can also aid in problem-solving. This technique can help us examine the problem from different perspectives and visualize the impacts of various solutions.

Exercise: When dealing with a problem, visualize it in your mind's eye. Try to see the problem from different angles. Then, visualize the potential solutions and their outcomes.

Think of Mike, a small business owner. His store's sales were dwindling, and he couldn't figure out why. He decided to use the Silva Method's visualization technique. He visualized his store and his customers, trying to see the situation from their perspective. This visualization led him to realize that his store layout was not customer-friendly, which could be discouraging potential customers. He then visualized various store layouts and imagined the customers' responses. Based on these visualizations, he redesigned his store, resulting in improved sales.

Positive Affirmations: Silva believed in the power of positive affirmations in problem-solving. Affirming to ourselves that we can find a solution helps boost our confidence and opens our mind to possible solutions.

Exercise: If a problem seems overwhelming, use positive affirmations. Say to yourself, "I have the ability to solve this problem. The solution is within me."

Take the example of Emily, a student struggling with mathematics. She had convinced herself that she was bad at it. She decided to apply Silva's positive affirmation technique. Every day, she told herself, "I am capable of understanding and excelling in mathematics." Over time, she noticed a significant improvement in her attitude towards math and her performance.

The Silva Method, with its unique focus on harnessing the subconscious mind, provides us with a fresh perspective on problem-solving. By practicing these techniques, you can improve your problem-solving skills and tackle issues more effectively. Remember, every problem has a solution within you – it's all about tapping into the power of your subconscious mind!

## 8.3 Success Stories and Practical Applications

The practical effectiveness of the Silva Method isn't just a theoretical proposition; it's borne out in the real world through the success stories of people who have implemented these techniques. From individuals overcoming personal obstacles to businesses achieving greater productivity, the method has positively influenced a variety of scenarios. In this section, we'll delve into some of these success stories and draw lessons on the method's practical applications.

Sarah, a high school teacher in Boston, had been struggling with chronic anxiety for years. Despite seeking professional help, she found her progress was slow and the issue persisted. It was only when she came across the Silva Method that she began to experience significant changes. She started with basic relaxation techniques, progressively calming her mind. Over time, she noticed her anxiety was lessening, replaced by a sense of calm and control. Sarah's story shows the power of the Silva Method in managing mental health challenges.

In the corporate world, a tech start-up in Silicon Valley, AptTech, was on the brink of failure, facing mounting losses and low employee morale. The leadership team turned to the Silva Method, primarily to address the latter issue. They organized regular visualization exercises and promoted positive affirmations across the company. Soon, there was a noticeable change in the overall atmosphere. Employee morale improved, creative solutions started flowing, and the company gradually began to turn around. AptTech's experience highlights the Silva Method's utility in a business context.

But the reach of the Silva Method is not just limited to mental health or business. For instance, Thomas, an amateur golfer, had plateaued and was struggling to improve his game. He decided to give the Silva Method a try. He began to visualize his swings, the trajectory of the ball, and even winning games. The result was phenomenal. Not only did he start performing better, but his confidence also soared, which positively impacted other aspects of his life. This illustrates how the method can enhance personal skills and hobbies.

The method also extends to academic success. Consider Emma, a university student who was finding it hard to concentrate on her studies. She used Silva's techniques to improve her focus and memory. She practiced visualization to remember complex concepts and used affirmations to boost her self-confidence. The result? Her grades significantly improved, and she developed a newfound love for learning.

These stories not only bring to life the impact of the Silva Method but also offer a glimpse into how versatile it is. These techniques can be applied to almost any area of life, from personal development and health to academic and professional success. By practicing these techniques, you too can create your success story.

However, it's important to remember that the journey with the Silva Method is personal. While these success stories can guide and inspire, your experience will be unique. You may face different challenges or achieve success in different areas. The key is to keep practicing, keep exploring, and remain open to the incredible potential of your mind.

# Chapter 10

## Mental and Physical Health

In the pursuit of well-being, we often tend to focus on either our physical health or mental health, rarely realizing the intricate link between the two. Our mind and body are intrinsically connected, operating in tandem, influencing and affecting each other in ways more profound than we realize. When our mind suffers, so does our body, and vice versa.

This chapter titled 'Mental and Physical Health' aims to shed light on this important correlation and how the Silva Method can aid in promoting holistic health. We will delve into the concept of the mind-body connection and understand the significant role it plays in our overall health. We will explore how the Silva Method, with its focus on mental control and positivity, can bring about improvements in both mental and physical health.

We will examine how the principles of the Silva Method can be applied to address health issues, to alleviate stress, and promote mental and physical well-being. From learning relaxation techniques to harnessing the power of positive visualization, we will uncover practical tools to elevate your health.

Lastly, we will review real-life case studies that demonstrate the impact of the Silva Method on individuals' health. These narratives will serve as tangible evidence of the transformative power of this method.

The journey to health does not have to be a lonely one. Join us as we navigate this exciting terrain, exploring the intersection of mind and body, and discovering how the Silva Method can guide us towards better health.

## 10.1 The Mind-Body Connection

We start our journey into understanding the intimate relationship between the mind and the body, a relationship that is often overlooked but is a crucial component of our overall well-being. This bond, often referred to as the mind-body connection, is an umbrella term encompassing the interactions between our thoughts, feelings, and behaviors and their impact on our physical health.

The origin of the mind-body connection lies in the fact that the mind is not confined to the brain but stretches across our entire body. Our thoughts and emotions don't just exist in our minds; they also manifest in our bodies, creating a two-way street of interaction and influence.

Think of the last time you felt butterflies in your stomach before a big presentation or noticed your heart racing during an intense movie scene. Or perhaps you've observed how a prolonged period of stress resulted in a tension headache or digestive issues. These are examples of how our mental state, whether it's thoughts or emotions, affects our physical health.

On the other hand, consider how your energy levels plummet when you are sick or how physical discomfort makes it harder to focus and think clearly. These examples illustrate how our physical state influences our mental health. This bi-directional communication between our mind and body is the essence of the mind-body connection.

The Silva Method, at its core, appreciates and leverages this connection. By gaining control over our mental state, we can indirectly affect our physical well-being, and vice versa.

The medical community's growing recognition of this relationship has led to a shift from treating mental and physical health separately towards a more holistic approach that acknowledges their interdependence. This understanding also opens the door for strategies that incorporate mental exercises, such as those provided by the Silva Method, into comprehensive healthcare plans.

The first step to utilizing the mind-body connection for health improvement is awareness. Being aware of this relationship means recognizing the signs our bodies are sending us and understanding how our thoughts and feelings might be influencing those signals.

Once we develop this awareness, we can use it to our advantage. By recognizing how our thoughts affect our bodies, we can learn to modify our thinking patterns, manage stress better, and cultivate a positive mental state that contributes to our physical health. This is where the Silva Method comes into play. It provides the tools to train your mind to positively influence your body, promote relaxation, and build resilience.

Additionally, understanding that our physical state can influence our mental health can encourage us to adopt healthier lifestyle habits. Physical exercise, balanced nutrition, and adequate sleep not only keep our bodies healthy but also have a profound effect on our mood, cognition, and overall mental health.

The Silva Method embraces the interplay between our mental and physical states. It uses mental exercises to help manage stress, reduce anxiety, and promote positive thinking, leading to physical health benefits. At the same time, it emphasizes the importance of maintaining physical health to foster a healthy mind.

In essence, the mind-body connection is a crucial aspect of our health that cannot be ignored. A holistic approach, one that acknowledges this connection and incorporates mental and physical health strategies, leads to better health outcomes. It's a journey that requires awareness, understanding, and active engagement in your health.

The Silva Method serves as a guide on this journey. By using its techniques, you can take control of your health, one thought, one emotion, one physical sensation at a time. It's about harnessing the power of your mind to heal your body and using your physical state to foster a healthy mind.

This fascinating interplay is what we'll continue to explore in the following sections. We'll dive into how you can use the Silva Method to maximize your health benefits by utilizing the mind-body connection. Remember, your mind and body are not separate entities but partners working together towards your overall well-being. As we explore the Silva Method in the context of mental and physical health, let this understanding be your guide.

## 10.2 Using The Silva Method for Mental and Physical Health

The Silva Method, with its roots in understanding and harnessing the mind's potential, can significantly contribute to both our mental and physical health. It's a gentle yet powerful approach that invites us to take control of our well-being through simple yet profound techniques. It's not just about alleviating symptoms or finding momentary relief. It's about diving deep into the realms of our minds to promote lasting changes and fostering resilience.

The first step in using the Silva Method for health is about establishing a strong foundation of relaxation. This might seem trivial in the face of more apparent health challenges like chronic pain, anxiety, or fatigue. However, it is in this state of deep relaxation that our bodies can kickstart their healing processes.

This relaxation process is achieved through the Alpha Level Exercises, which guides you into a state of deep physical and mental relaxation. When our bodies are relaxed, the heart rate slows, blood pressure decreases, and the production of stress hormones is reduced. This physical state promotes healing, reduces wear and tear on the body, and improves our immune function.

By integrating this relaxation exercise into your daily routine, you could potentially improve your body's resilience and ability to cope with physical stressors. More importantly, you also create an environment conducive for your mind to work on healing your body.

With this foundation of relaxation, the Silva Method then introduces the idea of using visualization and affirmations for health improvement. These techniques have been shown to influence physical health positively, primarily through their impact on the mind-body connection.

In visualization, you mentally picture your body as healthy, vibrant, and functioning optimally. You visualize your body healing, and you observe this healing in your mind's eye. This process is far from mere daydreaming. It's about intentionally creating images that support your health goals.

As for affirmations, they are statements that you mentally or verbally repeat to yourself, reinforcing the health outcomes you desire. They could be as simple as "My body heals quickly and efficiently" or as specific as "Every day, my [specific body part or function] becomes stronger and healthier." The key here is to phrase these affirmations in the present tense, suggesting the desired outcome is happening now.

These methods work by utilizing our mind's natural tendency to work towards what it perceives as its reality. By visualizing health and repeating affirmations, we feed our minds with images and statements that support health, encouraging our bodies to align with this vision.

While using the Silva Method for mental health, one significant component is managing stress and anxiety. The Alpha Level Exercises not only promote relaxation but also help manage stress, a significant contributor to numerous mental health challenges.

Additionally, the Three Scenes Technique provides a structured way to deal with worries, fears, and stressful scenarios. It allows you to mentally rehearse challenging situations and visualize positive outcomes, building your mental resilience and equipping you better to handle real-life stressors.

Remember, the Silva Method is not about replacing conventional healthcare. It's about supplementing it. It's about giving you tools that you can use along with your regular health care to support your healing and well-being.

## 10.3 Case Studies of Health Improvements with The Silva Method

We humans love stories. They bring information to life and make abstract ideas more tangible. So, let's discover the effectiveness of the Silva Method through real-life case studies, showing how people have used this technique to improve their health and well-being.

Our first case study revolves around a woman named Jane. Jane, a 48-year-old working mother, had been living with hypertension for years. Her busy life had left her with little time for relaxation and self-care. The medication helped, but she wanted a long-term solution that was more sustainable and healthy. That's when Jane discovered the Silva Method. She was particularly drawn to the Alpha Level Exercises and practiced them daily. Over time, Jane reported a significant decrease in her blood pressure levels, and her overall anxiety had reduced as well. The deep relaxation offered by the Silva Method had become a valuable ally in her battle against hypertension.

Our next story features Ben, a 30-year-old graphic designer, who had been struggling with insomnia. Despite trying various remedies, sleep remained elusive. When Ben stumbled upon the Silva Method, he was intrigued by the possibilities of visualization and decided to give it a try. Night after night, as he lay in bed, Ben would visualize himself sleeping peacefully. He also used positive affirmations, repeating to himself, "I sleep easily and deeply each night". Gradually, these practices began to work. Ben started to fall asleep faster and the quality of his sleep improved. No longer at the mercy of insomnia, Ben had gained control over his sleep patterns, thanks to the Silva Method.

The final case study features Karen, a woman in her early sixties, who was grappling with arthritic pain. With the Silva Method, Karen discovered a way to manage her discomfort without solely depending on medication. She began visualizing her joints as flexible and pain-free and combined this with affirmations like "My joints are healthy and pain-free". Over a period, Karen reported a decrease in the frequency and intensity of her pain. She credited the Silva Method as being instrumental in this improvement.

Each of these stories underscores the transformative power of the Silva Method. They highlight how this method can be used as a tool to support and improve our health, both physical and mental. The Silva Method isn't a magic wand, and it doesn't promise immediate results. What it offers is a set of skills that, when practiced diligently, can facilitate healthier living.

It's important to remember that these stories aren't exceptions. They can be your story too. Imagine a life where you are in control of your health, where you have the power to influence your well-being. That's what the Silva Method can offer. So, as we continue our journey, remember Jane, Ben, and Karen. They started as individuals seeking help, just like you. And they discovered, with the Silva Method, that the path to better health was not beyond reach, but within them, in the power of their minds.

# Chapter 11

## Manifestation and the Law of Attraction

Have you ever wondered why certain people seem to attract success and abundance effortlessly, while others struggle? It's no magic trick or secret society; it's the Law of Attraction in action. This principle states that like attracts like. It's the concept that our thoughts, both conscious and unconscious, impact our reality.

When it comes to the Law of Attraction, think of your mind as a powerful magnet. The energy you send out to the universe through your thoughts and feelings is what you attract back into your life. If you focus on positive thoughts, you will draw positive experiences. Conversely, if you let negative thoughts take control, you are likely to attract less favorable circumstances.

This chapter will illuminate the concept of manifestation and how it ties into the Law of Attraction. Manifestation is the process of transforming your thoughts, dreams, and desires into reality. It's the practice of aligning yourself with your desires and working towards them, ultimately allowing the universe to deliver.

But how does this align with the Silva Method? You see, the Silva Method empowers you to exercise control over your thoughts, harnessing your mental power to set the stage for effective manifestation. By learning to master your mind, you can manifest your desires, using the Law of Attraction to draw success, health, wealth, love, and more into your life.

We'll explore techniques for manifesting your desires and attracting abundance, bringing theoretical concepts into the realm of practical, everyday applications. You'll learn how to replace negative thought patterns with positive ones, tune into your intuition, and use visualization techniques to manifest your desires.

Throughout this chapter, we'll highlight real-life success stories of individuals who have used these methods to transform their lives. Their journeys will demonstrate how these principles work in practice, and hopefully inspire you to unlock your full mental potential. Together, we'll discover how you can harness the Silva Method and the Law of Attraction to create the life you desire and deserve. Let's begin.

## 11.1 The Concept of Manifestation and the Law of Attraction

Imagine you're in a garden filled with countless seeds. Each seed holds the potential to sprout into a vibrant plant, be it a robust tree, a delicate flower, or a lush vegetable. But this transformation doesn't happen spontaneously; it needs the right conditions: fertile soil, water, sunlight, and time. Now, think of your mind as this garden and your thoughts as these seeds.

Every thought you have, every dream you conjure up, and every desire you yearn for can sprout into reality, provided they're nurtured in the fertile ground of a positive, focused mind. This is the essence of manifestation: the process by which our internal thoughts, feelings, and beliefs shape our external reality. It's not about merely wishing or dreaming; it's about believing, focusing, and taking aligned action.

Now, let's connect this idea with the Law of Attraction, a universal principle asserting that like attracts like. To put it simply, the energy you emit into the world, through your thoughts and feelings, attracts similar energy back to you. In the context of our garden analogy, the Law of Attraction determines what kinds of plants will grow. If you water your seeds of ambition, positivity, and gratitude, you'll grow a garden of success, happiness, and abundance. But if you water your seeds of doubt, negativity, and fear, you're likely to cultivate a garden of obstacles, disappointment, and scarcity.

It's crucial to realize that the Law of Attraction is always in operation, whether you're aware of it or not. Just like gravity, it doesn't switch off. It's continuously influencing your life, attracting circumstances, relationships, and experiences that mirror your dominant thoughts and feelings.

The beautiful union of manifestation and the Law of Attraction can be harnessed using the Silva Method. This method equips you with techniques to control your thoughts, thereby influencing what you attract into your life. The power of your mind, once honed and directed, becomes the architect of your reality. It constructs your world, brick by brick, thought by thought, belief by belief.

For instance, let's say you're striving for a promotion at work. By applying the Silva Method, you first quiet your mind, entering the relaxed, focused state of Alpha level. In this state, your mind is at its most potent, ready to seed your goal. You clearly visualize your desired outcome - seeing yourself thriving in your new role, feeling the satisfaction of your accomplishment. By regularly nurturing this vision with belief and positive emotion, you set the stage for manifestation.

Simultaneously, you're applying the Law of Attraction. By focusing your energy on success and fulfillment, you're aligning with these frequencies. The universe, akin to a giant mirror, reflects this energy back to you, drawing opportunities and experiences into your life that match your internal state. Over time, as you maintain this focus and take inspired action, you increase your chances of manifesting your promotion.

This process is not confined to career goals; it applies to all areas of your life. Whether you desire better health, more meaningful relationships, financial abundance, or personal growth, the principles remain the same. By consciously controlling your thoughts using the Silva Method, and understanding the Law of Attraction, you become a proactive gardener of your life. You decide which seeds to water, which plants to nurture, and what kind of garden you wish to cultivate.

However, it's important to keep in mind that manifestation isn't a quick-fix solution or an escape route from challenges. Life will still present difficulties, and not every seed will sprout. But with your newfound understanding, you can navigate these challenges differently. You can see them as opportunities for growth rather than roadblocks. You can choose to respond with resilience and optimism, further reinforcing your positive energy, and attracting better outcomes.

We're just beginning to scratch the surface of this remarkable union of manifestation and the Law of Attraction. We'll explore more deeply in the following sections, learning effective techniques and understanding their practical application. As we journey together, remember that this is a process, not an event. Be patient with yourself, keep an open mind, and trust the process. You are not merely learning;

you're transforming, evolving, and blossoming into a more empowered version of yourself.

## 11.2 Techniques to Manifest Desires and Attract Abundance

Have you ever noticed how a radio works? It's all about tuning into the right frequency to receive a clear signal. This simple device holds a lesson for us in manifesting our desires and attracting abundance. By tuning our minds to the right 'frequency,' we can send clear signals to the universe about our intentions and desires.

In this section, we will explore three powerful techniques based on the Silva Method that will help you do just that: Visualization, Emotionalization, and Affirmation. We will then follow with an integrative process that combines all three, creating a potent tool for manifestation.

Let's begin.

Visualization

If the mind is the garden and our thoughts the seeds, visualization is the act of clearly picturing the sprouting plant. It is more than daydreaming; it is the purposeful act of creating detailed mental images of your desires as if they have already come to fruition.

Using the Silva Method, start your visualization practice by entering the Alpha level, a deeply relaxed state where your mind is most receptive. Here, you visualize your desired outcome in vivid detail. If you desire a new job, for instance, don't just picture yourself in a new office. Feel the fabric of the office chair, hear the clickety-clack of the keyboard, smell the fresh coffee from the breakroom. The more senses you involve, the more real it becomes to your mind.

Emotionalization

Visualization creates the picture; emotionalization infuses it with life. It is the process of attaching positive emotions to your visualized desires. The stronger the emotion, the stronger the signal you send to the universe.

To practice emotionalization, return to your vivid mental image, and imagine the feelings that come with it. Continuing the new job example, imagine the pride of success, the exhilaration of achievement, the joy of doing what you love. Feel these emotions in the present, as if your goal is already achieved. This technique, in essence, tricks your brain into believing that your vision is your reality, and consequently, it works to align your actions towards that reality.

Affirmation

Words are powerful. They can create, they can destroy, and they can transform. Affirmation uses this power to strengthen your manifestation efforts. It involves using positive, present tense statements that describe your desired outcome.

Once again, use the Silva Method to enter the Alpha level. Then, begin to recite your affirmations. For the new job, an affirmation could be, "I am enjoying my new job where I am valued and successful." It's important that your affirmations are personal, positive, and stated in the present tense. Repeat them daily, letting them sink into your subconscious mind.

Now that we've looked at the individual techniques let's explore an integrative practice that weaves them together into a potent tool for manifestation and attracting abundance.

The Silva Manifestation Technique

Enter the Alpha Level: Begin by getting into a comfortable position, taking deep breaths, and gradually relaxing your body. As you learn to do this, you will find it easier to enter the Alpha level.

Set Your Intent: Clearly state what you want to manifest. It could be a goal, an object, a state of being. Be as precise as possible.

Visualize: Once in the Alpha level, begin to visualize your desire. Create a mental movie, adding as many sensory details as possible.

Emotionalize: Infuse your visualization with emotion. Feel the joy, satisfaction, or love that comes with achieving your desire. The more intense the emotion, the more powerful the manifestation.

Affirm: Create a positive, present tense statement that represents your desire and start repeating it in your mind. Believe in the words you are saying.

Release and Trust: After spending some time in this state, gently bring yourself back to your normal consciousness. Release your desire to the universe and trust that it will manifest in its own time.

Learning to manifest desires and attract abundance is not a quick fix. It requires practice, patience, and above all, belief in yourself and the process. However, by consistently applying these techniques, you will start to notice changes, both subtle and significant, in your reality. As with any skill, proficiency comes with practice. The more you engage with these techniques, the more adept you will become at harnessing your inherent power to shape your reality.

Remember, we are not trying to control the universe, but aligning ourselves with its abundance. In doing so, we create the conditions for our desires to manifest and for prosperity to flow into our lives. It's like sailing - you can't change the wind, but you can adjust your sails. Here's to your journey towards abundance, may it be filled with joy and discovery.

## 11.3 Real Life Success Stories and Applications

In this part of our journey, we will turn the spotlight onto some real-life narratives, where individuals have leveraged the power of manifestation and the law of attraction to reshape their realities. Their stories echo the potential of the human mind and show us the tangible effects of these practices in action.

Story 1: The Entrepreneur's Vision

Let's begin with the story of Lisa, a young entrepreneur. Lisa dreamed of starting her own marketing agency but was struggling to get her business off the ground. She faced financial issues, lack of resources, and self-doubt.

To combat these challenges, Lisa turned to the Silva Manifestation Technique. She started visualizing her agency as a success, seeing a team working with her, happy clients, and a healthy bank balance. She associated positive emotions with this visualization, feeling the joy of accomplishment, the thrill of leadership, and the satisfaction of financial security. Lisa affirmed her vision daily with the statement, "I am running a successful marketing agency."

Over time, Lisa's actions began to mirror her visualization. She networked more confidently, found resources she previously overlooked, and gradually built her team. Within a year, her agency turned profitable. Lisa's story exemplifies the power of visualizing success and aligning actions with that vision.

Story 2: The Writer's Breakthrough

Next, we meet David, an aspiring writer struggling to finish his first novel. Burdened by writer's block and doubt, he felt like giving up.

David decided to try the techniques he'd heard about. Every morning, he visualized himself typing the last sentence of his novel, hearing the sound of the keys, feeling the relief and joy of completion. He attached these positive emotions to his visualization, and affirmed his vision with the statement, "I am a successful novelist."

Gradually, David's block began to lift. Ideas flowed freely, and his self-doubt decreased. After six months, he typed the last sentence of his novel just as he had visualized. He found a publisher shortly after, marking his breakthrough as a professional writer. His story underlines the impact of aligning emotional energy with one's goals.

Story 3: The Homemaker's Happiness

Our final story is about Emily, a homemaker feeling unfulfilled and unhappy. She yearned for joy but didn't know how to find it.

Emily started using the Silva Method, visualizing herself as joyful and content. She associated feelings of happiness, love, and contentment with her visualization and affirmed her vision with the phrase, "I am full of joy and satisfaction."

Over the next few months, Emily noticed changes in her attitude and perspective. She found happiness in small, everyday things and discovered new hobbies that brought her joy. She began to reflect the joyful person she had visualized. Emily's transformation shows us that manifesting isn't always about tangible items or clear-cut goals; it can also be about states of being.

These narratives serve as testaments to the transformative power of manifestation and the law of attraction. They underscore the magic that unfolds when we align our thoughts, emotions, and actions with our desires. Whether it's building a successful business, completing a novel, or finding personal happiness, the Silva Method provides a practical roadmap for manifesting our deepest desires. As these stories show, our minds hold the potential to shape our reality. When we dare to dream and believe in those dreams, we open the door to endless possibilities.

# CHAPTER 12
# Advanced Silva Method Techniques

Our mental journey up to this point has prepared us for the exciting vistas that await us. You have learned about the importance of beliefs, harnessing your intuition, and the basic techniques of the Silva Method. You are not the same person you were when you began this journey - your mind has expanded, your consciousness has deepened, and your understanding of yourself has grown. This newfound understanding serves as the foundation for the advanced Silva Method techniques that we will explore in this chapter.

These techniques take you beyond the surface level of your mind and into its most profound depths. As we dive into these advanced methods, remember that the purpose is to enhance your life and the lives of those around you. The power that you are cultivating within your mind should be used responsibly, with wisdom and empathy.

## 12.1 Accessing the Collective Consciousness

It's easy to view ourselves as independent beings, isolated entities in a sea of other individuals. Yet, beneath the surface, beneath our individual consciousness, a current flows that connects us all - the collective consciousness.

The concept of collective consciousness has been contemplated by philosophers and scientists alike, each seeking to comprehend the unseen threads that connect the human experience. In the words of eminent psychologist Carl Jung, the collective consciousness is "a kind of universal psyche that is present in every individual". It's a repository of shared wisdom, experiences, and ideas that permeate humanity, irrespective of race, culture, or geographical location.

Accessing this collective consciousness can provide a profound sense of connection, a realization that we are part of something much larger than ourselves. It can also offer insight, inspiration, and wisdom, a virtual library of human experience and knowledge that can guide us through our own lives. How can we, using the Silva Method, tap into this reservoir of shared human consciousness?

First, we must understand that accessing the collective consciousness is not about trying to forcibly pierce a veil or crack open a locked door. It's about quieting the mind, about moving past the noise and chatter of our individual consciousness and into the tranquil depths of our shared human psyche. It involves moving from a state of 'doing' to a state of 'being', where we simply exist in the moment, open, receptive, and connected.

One way to facilitate this transition is through deep meditation. As you relax your mind and body, visualize yourself as part of a vast network, a web of human consciousness that spans the globe. Imagine your thoughts, feelings, and experiences mingling with those of every other human being, forming a tapestry of collective experience and wisdom.

This visual exercise is not just metaphorical but is a symbolic representation of the state you're trying to achieve - a state of connectedness with all of humanity. As you hold this image in your mind, allow yourself to simply 'be', letting go of any thoughts or distractions that arise.

In this state of deep meditation and connectedness, you may find that insights and ideas spontaneously arise. These could be the fruits of your connection to the collective consciousness - wisdom from the collective human experience manifesting in your own mind. It's essential to approach these insights with an open mind and a humble heart, recognizing them as gifts from our shared human journey.

As you continue to practice this technique, you'll find it becomes easier to enter this state of connectedness. The barriers that separate us will seem less solid, less real. You'll begin to view the world, not just from your perspective but from the perspective of humanity as a whole. This expanded perspective can lead to increased empathy, understanding, and wisdom, enriching not only your life but the lives of those around you as well.

Remember, the collective consciousness is not a distant realm to be visited but a fundamental part of who we are. Accessing it does not require special skills or talents but simply an open mind, a quiet heart, and a willingness to connect with the shared human experience. Through the Silva Method, you can tap into this shared consciousness, enriching your life with the wisdom of humanity and deepening your connection with the world around you.

## 12.2 The Power of Mind Control

Often, when we hear the term 'mind control,' we conjure images of mysterious figures swaying others to act against their will. Yet, the truth is far less sinister and more empowering. When we talk about mind control here, we're discussing self-mastery—the ability to guide and shape our thoughts, emotions, and reactions in service to our highest good.

Your mind is an extraordinarily powerful tool, one that shapes your reality more than any other factor. It's the lens through which you perceive the world, the architect of your emotions, and the driving force behind your actions. Yet, for many of us, our minds often feel like a wild horse, running amok with unchecked thoughts, overwhelming emotions, and impulsive reactions.

Mind control, as taught in the Silva Method, is about taking the reins of this wild horse, not to subdue or dominate it, but to guide it gently yet firmly towards your chosen path. It's about understanding the power of your thoughts, harnessing the energy of your emotions, and directing your actions towards your goals. Let's explore the three main aspects of mind control: thoughts, emotions, and actions.

First, let's discuss thoughts. Our thoughts are not random; they are a direct response to our beliefs, experiences, and perceptions. By changing our thinking patterns, we can significantly influence our reality. How can we accomplish this? It begins by observing your thought patterns, identifying the negative or limiting beliefs, and consciously replacing them with more positive, empowering ones. This process of self-awareness and conscious thought replacement can dramatically shift your mental landscape, leading to greater positivity, resilience, and motivation.

Next, we move onto emotions. Emotions are powerful—they can inspire us to great heights or pull us down into the depths of despair. Yet, we often let our emotions control us, reacting impulsively without considering the consequences. Mind control involves understanding our emotions, recognizing them as valuable signals, and learning to respond to them constructively. It's about not letting temporary emotions dictate long-term decisions, instead, using them as indicators to guide our responses. This emotional mastery can lead to greater mental and emotional stability, improved relationships, and enhanced personal growth.

Finally, we address actions. Every action we take is a manifestation of our thoughts and emotions. By controlling our mind, we can direct our actions towards our goals and aspirations, rather than being led astray by temporary impulses or distractions. This involves developing discipline, setting clear goals, and taking consistent action towards these goals. When our actions are aligned with our values and aspirations, we experience greater success, fulfillment, and satisfaction in life.

Harnessing the power of mind control is not an overnight process; it requires practice, patience, and persistence. Yet, the rewards are immense. As you learn to guide your thoughts, manage your emotions, and direct your actions, you'll notice a profound shift in your life. You'll feel more confident, more in control, and more equipped to face life's challenges. You'll also be better positioned to achieve your goals and realize your full potential.

Remember, the power to shape your life lies within you, within your mind. By learning to control your mind, you're not just mastering a set of techniques; you're embarking on a journey of self-discovery and personal empowerment. With the Silva Method as your guide, you have all the tools you need to harness the power of mind control and take the reins of your life.

## 12.3 Implementing Silva Method in Everyday Life

The beauty of the Silva Method is not confined to the principles and techniques themselves but rather how seamlessly they integrate into everyday life. Let's illustrate how the Silva Method isn't something that you practice for a few minutes each day, but rather a way of life that informs every thought, action, and interaction.

Morning Meditation: How you start your day sets the tone for the rest of it. A Silva Method morning meditation can help you align your mind with positivity and focus. It can be as simple as spending a few minutes in quiet contemplation, visualizing your day unfolding exactly as you want it to, feeling the emotions of success, joy, and fulfillment that come with it. Such a practice calibrates your mind to expect positive outcomes, thus setting you on a path for success each day.

Mindful Eating: The act of eating is so automatic that we often do it mindlessly, hardly tasting or enjoying the food. The Silva Method encourages mindfulness in all activities, including eating. Savor each bite, tune into the flavors, and appreciate the nourishment you're receiving. This practice encourages gratitude and promotes healthier eating habits.

Centering During Challenges: Life is not without its challenges. Stressful situations, challenging interactions, or setbacks can throw us off balance. By using Silva Method's centering technique, you can quickly return to a state of balance and peace. This involves taking a few deep breaths, reconnecting with your inner self, and reminding yourself of your innate capacity to handle any situation.

Positive Affirmations: Words carry energy, and the messages we send to ourselves can influence our mental and emotional states. By regularly repeating positive affirmations, you can reshape your belief system and elevate your mindset. These could be general affirmations such as "I am capable and resilient," or specific ones aligned with your personal goals.

Decision-Making with Intuition: We all face decisions daily, from minor ones like what to wear or eat, to major ones like career moves or financial investments. The Silva Method encourages us to harness our intuition in decision-making, promoting choices that align with our deepest wisdom and highest good.

Visualizing Success: Whether you're working on a personal project, preparing for an important presentation, or pursuing a long-term goal, visualization is a powerful tool. By creating a vivid mental image of the successful outcome, you're aligning your subconscious mind with your conscious goals, thus increasing the likelihood of their realization.

Nighttime Reflection: Just as the morning meditation sets the tone for your day, a nighttime reflection helps you process your experiences, celebrate your victories, learn from your challenges, and release any negative emotions. It's an opportunity to thank yourself for the efforts of the day and to align with peace and gratitude before sleep.

Each of these practices is a strand in the fabric of your daily life, each reinforcing and supporting the others. By incorporating the Silva Method into your everyday routines, you're not only enhancing your life on a day-to-day basis but also building a strong foundation for long-term growth, success, and fulfillment. You're creating a life where the power of your mind is not an abstract concept but a living, breathing reality that you experience every single day.

And therein lies the true power of the Silva Method. It's not just about learning techniques; it's about transforming your life, from the inside out. It's about experiencing the magic that happens when you align with your mind's power and allow it to guide you towards your highest potential. And that journey, my friends, is one that can start right here, right now, in the very midst of your everyday life.

## 12.4 The Way Forward: Taking Control of Your Mind's Power

Taking control of your mind's power is like embarking on a journey of self-discovery and transformation. It's a journey that goes beyond the ordinary and stretches into the extraordinary realms of the mind. It's a journey that's filled with discovery, growth, and a wealth of experiences that bring forth your best self. The path may be challenging at times, but with the Silva Method as your guide, you're equipped to navigate it effectively.

Continuous Learning: Adopting the Silva Method is a beginning, not an end. The richness and depth of this method provide for a lifetime of exploration and learning. Consider this: the human mind is the most complex and sophisticated entity we know of, and you've embarked on a journey to understand and master it. Keep your curiosity alive, and continue to learn and grow. Make it a lifelong quest to understand your mind better and to harness its power more effectively.

Consistent Practice: The effectiveness of the Silva Method lies in its regular application. The more you practice, the more familiar you become with your mind's workings and the more adept you become at navigating its depths. Consider the analogy of learning a new musical instrument. It's through consistent practice that you develop proficiency. The same is true for mastering your mind. Keep practicing the techniques, and you'll see progress.

**Personalized Approach:** The Silva Method is highly flexible and adaptable. While it offers a framework and specific techniques, you're encouraged to adapt them to suit your individual needs, preferences, and lifestyle. It's your journey, and you're the best judge of what works best for you. Experiment, adapt, and make the method your own.

**Application in Real Life:** Learning the Silva Method is not just about the time you spend practicing the techniques. It's also about applying what you've learned in your day-to-day life. Every interaction, every decision, every challenge, and every celebration is an opportunity to apply your newfound knowledge and skills. It's in these real-life applications that you'll see the true power of the Silva Method.

**Community Support:** Don't underestimate the power of community. Joining a group of like-minded individuals who are also practicing the Silva Method can be an excellent source of motivation, support, and shared learning. Whether it's an online forum, a local group, or a global event, connect with others who are on the same journey. Share your experiences, learn from theirs, and grow together.

**Reflection and Adaptation:** As you walk this path, take time to reflect on your experiences. What's working well for you? What challenges are you encountering? How are you growing and evolving? Reflection not only provides insights but also helps you adapt your approach based on your experiences and needs. It's an integral part of your journey.

Patience and Kindness: Finally, be patient with yourself. Mastering your mind's power is not an overnight endeavor. There will be times of rapid progress, times of slow and steady growth, and times when it feels like you're not moving at all. During all these times, be kind to yourself. Celebrate your victories, learn from your setbacks, and keep moving forward.

The way forward, dear reader, is a journey of fascinating discoveries and inspiring growth. It's a journey that is as unique as you are. It's a journey that takes courage, commitment, and curiosity. But most importantly, it's a journey that leads to the greatest destination of all - a life lived with the full power and potential of your incredible mind. So step forward with confidence, knowing that the Silva Method is your trusted companion on this remarkable journey.

# Chapter 13

## The Legacy of José Silva and the Silva Method-basic intro

Jose Silva was not just a man; he was a visionary, a pioneer who sought to unlock the full potential of the human mind. His innovative ideas, his relentless pursuit of knowledge, and his unwavering belief in human potential led to the creation of the Silva Method. This method, born from a unique blend of science and spirituality, has transformed countless lives across the globe, creating a legacy that continues to grow even today.

The story of Jose Silva and the Silva Method is one of perseverance, ingenuity, and the power of the human spirit. Born into poverty in Laredo, Texas, Silva's early life was marked by hardship. But it was these very challenges that ignited his unyielding spirit, his determination to rise above his circumstances, and his unwavering belief in the boundless potential of the human mind.

Jose Silva's journey towards the creation of the Silva Method began in earnest when he started researching ways to improve his children's grades. His studies in psychology, hypnosis, and the human brain, coupled with his intuitive understanding of the mind's potential, led to the development of a method that could maximize the brain's capabilities. The Silva Method was born.

This method, marked by its simplicity and effectiveness, has had an undeniable impact on millions of people across the globe. Its principles have been taught in over 110 countries, translated into dozens of languages, and embraced by people from all walks of life.

In the coming sections, we will explore the global impact of the Silva Method, delve into the work of Silva International, and discuss how Silva's vision continues to guide the method's evolution. This is not just a story of a method or a man; it is a testament to the power of the human mind, a celebration of our potential to transform our lives and the world around us.

Jose Silva once said, "You can learn to use more of your mind to help you achieve your goals in life." His life and his legacy are a testament to this belief. As you navigate the pages of this chapter, you will not only learn about the incredible legacy of Jose Silva and the Silva Method but also feel inspired to tap into your own potential, to harness the power of your mind, and to shape your own destiny.

## 13.1. The global impact of the Silva Method

The global impact of the Silva Method is an enduring testament to the transformative power of Jose Silva's innovative ideas. Over time, this approach has made its way to millions, crossed boundaries of cultures, languages, and nations, and transcended barriers to leave a lasting imprint on the canvas of human potential.

Originating in a humble Texas household, the Silva Method was never confined by geographical boundaries. From its early beginnings, it broke free from its local origins, reaching out to touch people's lives, irrespective of their location. Even as we speak, the Silva Method is taught in more than 110 countries, translated into dozens of languages, and embraced by millions around the world.

This vast reach did not occur by accident. It was the result of Jose Silva's unwavering belief that the human mind's potential is universal. His vision transcended boundaries of race, religion, and nationality. He believed in a world where everyone, regardless of their background, could tap into their latent mental abilities, unlocking a reservoir of untapped potential to enhance their quality of life.

The Silva Method has indeed made significant strides on the global stage. Its simple yet powerful techniques have found resonance across diverse cultures, making it a universal language of human potential. The techniques taught in the Silva Method, like creative visualization, meditation, and positive thinking, have become mainstream ideas, influencing countless lives and changing the way people think about their abilities.

The global acceptance and recognition of the Silva Method are further reinforced by its adoption in various fields. In the world of sports, for instance, many athletes have used the Silva Method to enhance their performance. They've harnessed the power of visualization and positive thinking to overcome challenges, improve focus, and boost their confidence. Likewise, in education, the Silva Method has helped students enhance their learning abilities, improve focus, and achieve academic success.

Similarly, in the corporate world, the Silva Method's principles have been integrated into training programs to improve productivity, enhance creativity, and boost employee morale. By harnessing the power of the mind, individuals and organizations have been able to create an environment conducive to success and growth.

Beyond its practical applications, the Silva Method's impact is also felt on a more profound, personal level. It has provided individuals with the tools to cope with stress, overcome fears, and deal with life's challenges more effectively. It has fostered personal growth, empowered individuals to take charge of their lives, and inspired them to strive for a better future.

The global footprint of the Silva Method is not just a measure of its physical reach. It's a reflection of its profound ability to transform lives, shape destinies, and unlock the immense potential of the human mind. As we continue to explore the world of the Silva Method, its powerful legacy and its potential to continue impacting lives around the globe, we invite you to open your mind and join this global journey of transformation.

## 13.2. Silva Method Today: Silva International

Silva International stands as a beacon of enlightenment in a world ever-thirsty for personal development, wellness, and the unlocking of human potential. It stands as the embodiment of Jose Silva's vision, a global organization dedicated to promoting and advancing the Silva Method on a universal scale.

The story of Silva International is a tale of resilience, passion, and a ceaseless commitment to human potential. Silva International was established after Jose Silva's passing to carry forward his legacy and keep the flame of his life's work burning brightly. It emerged as a stalwart advocate for the Silva Method, an institution committed to spreading Silva's teachings, preserving their purity, and continuing the journey that Silva began over five decades ago.

In essence, Silva International is more than just an organization; it is the heart that pumps life into the body of the Silva Method, keeping it alive and vibrant. Today, the organization is the primary vehicle for the global delivery of the Silva Method's teachings, providing a structured framework for its propagation and ensuring that it reaches all corners of the globe.

Through a network of certified Silva Method trainers, Silva International ensures that the method is taught accurately and effectively. These trainers, chosen for their deep understanding of the Silva Method and their passion for teaching, are the torchbearers of Silva's vision. They carry his teachings forward, illuminating the path for millions worldwide who seek to harness their mind's power and realize their potential.

One of the key objectives of Silva International is to ensure that the Silva Method remains relevant and adaptable to changing times. The world is continually evolving, and with it, the challenges and needs of individuals. Silva International is dedicated to fine-tuning and updating the Silva Method, making sure it remains responsive to these changing needs, without deviating from its core principles.

To this end, Silva International actively engages in research and development. Collaborating with experts and researchers in the field of mind science, the organization continually explores new ways to enhance and expand the Silva Method. This commitment to research and innovation is a testament to Silva International's dedication to keeping the Silva Method at the forefront of personal development and mind science.

Moreover, Silva International has taken the Silva Method beyond individual wellness and personal growth. Recognizing the potential of the Silva Method in improving organizational efficiency and fostering a healthier work environment, Silva International offers corporate training programs. These programs introduce companies to the power of the Silva Method, helping them improve productivity, enhance creativity, and foster a positive work culture.

In a world growing more interconnected every day, Silva International understands the importance of a robust online presence. To this end, it offers online courses, webinars, and a range of digital resources. This ensures that anyone, anywhere in the world, can learn the Silva Method, regardless of their location.

## 13.3. Continuing Silva's vision

As we stand on the precipice of the future, the legacy of José Silva resonates stronger than ever before. His vision, brought to life in the Silva Method, continues to impact lives globally, illuminating the path of countless individuals in their quest for self-realization and personal growth.

Yet, the journey does not end here. Just as José Silva relentlessly pursued the unlocking of human potential during his lifetime, the task before us now is to continue this pursuit, to nurture and grow his vision. There are still mountains to scale, frontiers to cross, and mysteries to unravel in the endless expanse of the human mind.

It is essential to remember that the core of Silva's vision was empowerment, the belief that each person has within them an immense untapped power, the power of their mind. Continuing his vision means reaffirming this belief, stoking the fires of empowerment, and fostering an environment where everyone has the tools to tap into this power.

One significant avenue for the continuation of Silva's vision is education. This goes beyond merely teaching the techniques of the Silva Method. It involves fostering a broader understanding of the mind, its potential, and the ways we can harness this potential. It means instilling a mindset that values introspection, mindfulness, and the pursuit of personal growth. This education can start early, incorporated into school curriculums, allowing children to build a strong foundation for understanding their minds and abilities.

Moreover, continuing Silva's vision involves ongoing research and development. As our understanding of the human mind evolves, so too should the Silva Method. Collaborating with psychologists, neuroscientists, and other experts in the field can lead to advancements and innovations in the method, enhancing its effectiveness and accessibility.

Another essential facet of continuing Silva's vision is reaching out to more diverse populations. The beauty of the Silva Method lies in its universal applicability - it transcends cultural, social, and geographical boundaries. Efforts should be geared towards making the Silva Method available and accessible to people from all walks of life, no matter where they are in the world. This includes translating the teachings into multiple languages, adapting the method to different cultural contexts, and leveraging technology to reach remote and underprivileged populations.

Lastly, Silva's vision was not limited to individual wellness. He believed in the positive ripple effects that empowered individuals can have on their families, communities, and society at large. Therefore, continuing his vision means taking the Silva Method beyond individual training and integrating it into various sectors of society, including businesses, schools, and community organizations. This approach can catalyze positive change on a broader scale, promoting collective wellness and growth.

# CHAPTER 14

# The Future of the Silva Method

The Silva Method, since its conception, has played a transformational role in the lives of countless individuals worldwide. But its journey is far from over. As we stand at the intersection of what has been and what is yet to come, it's time to turn our gaze toward the future—A future where the Silva Method continues to evolve, adapt, and influence the course of human potential.

## 14.1. Modern Adaptations and Advancements

As we step into the modern era of the Silva Method, one thing remains clear - its principles have endured, proving their timeless relevance. Yet, even as these core principles stay unchanged, their application and methodologies have evolved significantly, mirroring our modern context and benefiting from technological advancements. Let's journey through some of the prominent adaptations and advancements that have defined the Silva Method's evolution in contemporary times.

One significant adaptation is the incorporation of digital platforms for learning and practicing the Silva Method. Gone are the days when practicing this technique required in-person classes or seminars. The advent of the digital age has allowed the Silva Method to break physical barriers, bringing the technique to every corner of the globe. Online courses, e-books, webinars, virtual workshops - these platforms have made the Silva Method accessible to millions who otherwise might not have had the opportunity.

The evolution of the Silva Method has also seen a closer integration with other cognitive and psychological practices. Modern adaptations have seen the Silva Method combined with elements of mindfulness, cognitive behavioral therapy (CBT), and even neuroscience research. This synthesis has given birth to programs designed not only for personal development but also for specific purposes like stress management, overcoming phobias, or enhancing creativity.

Artificial Intelligence (AI) has also been instrumental in driving the recent advancements in the Silva Method. Through AI-driven apps, individuals now have access to personalized Silva Method training programs. These apps can adapt to individual progress and preferences, making the practice of the Silva Method more tailored than ever before. For example, if a user struggles with a specific technique, the app can provide additional exercises and guidance to help them master it.

Additionally, Virtual Reality (VR) and Augmented Reality (AR) technologies have added an entirely new dimension to the practice. These technologies can simulate environments that facilitate better practice of the Silva Method techniques. Imagine practicing visualization in a VR world tailored to stimulate your senses and enhance your imaginative capabilities - this is no longer science fiction, but a reality that is transforming how we practice the Silva Method.

Finally, the Silva Method's adaptability has also seen it incorporated into corporate training programs. Companies have begun to recognize the value of mental training for improving productivity, creativity, and employee wellbeing. The Silva Method, with its emphasis on visualization and mental discipline, has found a significant place in these corporate wellness programs.

## 14.2 Predictions and Hopes for the Future

Just as the Silva Method has evolved and adapted in the present, so it will continue to shape-shift and grow in the future. While we can't say for certain what form these changes will take, we can, with confidence, share our predictions and hopes for what lies ahead. Let's venture into the landscape of possibilities and allow our imaginations to unfold the potential future of the Silva Method.

A crucial prediction for the Silva Method's future lies in its potential to become even more integrated into our educational systems. Imagine a world where children from a young age are equipped with the mental tools to deal with stress, enhance their learning capabilities, and master the art of visualization and goal-setting. The Silva Method could transform education by emphasizing not just intellectual growth, but holistic mental development.

Following on this thread, we see the Silva Method playing an increasingly important role in mental health support. As our understanding of mental health continues to deepen, techniques like the Silva Method that promote self-awareness, mindfulness, and positive visualization could become fundamental aspects of therapeutic processes.

With technology advancing at a rapid pace, we can expect to see more sophisticated uses of AI, VR, and AR in the practice of the Silva Method. We envision AI-powered coaches that not only guide users through techniques but also understand their emotions and respond accordingly. As for VR and AR, they could become even more immersive, providing users with extraordinarily lifelike environments to practice visualization and mental rehearsal.

Another exciting frontier is the integration of the Silva Method with biofeedback devices. Such devices can monitor bodily functions like heart rate and brain waves in real-time. By linking these devices to the Silva Method, individuals could receive instant feedback on their practice, helping them to understand and improve their mental states more effectively.

While these are predictions grounded in trends and developments we see today, let's also explore our hopes for the Silva Method's future. We hope that the Silva Method will become more universally recognized as a potent tool for mental development. We hope to see more scientific research validating its techniques and adding to its credibility.

Above all, our most profound hope is that the Silva Method will continue to empower individuals. We hope it continues to guide people to reach their fullest potential, helping them to transform their lives and, in turn, the world around them. It's a grand vision, but then again, the Silva Method has always been about dreaming big and turning those dreams into reality.

As we reflect on these predictions and hopes, we realize the future of the Silva Method is not set in stone. It's a living, evolving entity, shaped by the needs of the people it serves and the world it inhabits. However, no matter how it changes or evolves, at its heart, the Silva Method will always remain a beacon guiding us towards greater mental freedom and empowerment.

## 14.3. How You Can Be Part of the Silva Method Future

The future of the Silva Method is not just about the practitioners, researchers, or technologists—it's also about you. As a reader of this book, you're already an important part of the Silva Method's story. Your commitment to learning and applying the techniques propels the method forward. As we look towards the future, your role can expand, and you can become a more active participant in the journey. Let's explore how you can contribute to the evolving story of the Silva Method.

Firstly, continue to learn and grow. This book has provided you with the foundational tools of the Silva Method, but don't stop here. Stay informed about the latest developments, further research, and updated techniques. As the Silva Method adapts to new discoveries and advances in fields like neuroscience, psychology, and technology, so should your practice. Embrace lifelong learning as part of your journey with the Silva Method.

Secondly, share your experiences. Your personal story has the power to inspire and motivate others. Whether it's a major life change you attribute to the Silva Method or smaller day-to-day improvements, don't underestimate the power of your narrative. Share your journey with friends, family, colleagues, and through online platforms dedicated to personal growth. By doing so, you're not just spreading awareness about the Silva Method but also contributing to a community that supports and learns from each other's experiences.

Next, consider teaching or mentoring. After mastering the Silva Method techniques, you may feel compelled to guide others on their journey. Teaching is a great way to deepen your own understanding while helping others discover their mental potential. If teaching feels like a big leap, start by mentoring someone close to you. Remember, guiding someone else can also be a powerful learning experience for you.

Involve the Silva Method in your professional life. Today, organizations across sectors recognize the importance of mental well-being, creativity, and problem-solving skills. If you're in a position to influence, advocate for integrating the Silva Method techniques into your organization's training programs. If you're an educator, explore how the Silva Method can benefit your students.

Participate in research. As we've seen, the Silva Method's future is intertwined with ongoing scientific research. If you have an opportunity to participate in studies, your contribution can help further our understanding of the Silva Method and its impact.

Lastly, innovate. As the Silva Method evolves, there's room for fresh ideas and creative applications. Don't hesitate to experiment with the techniques, applying them in new contexts, or combining them with other approaches you find beneficial. Your innovations could become part of the Silva Method's growth story.

To be part of the Silva Method's future is to be an active participant in shaping your mental landscape and, by extension, the world around you. It's about contributing to a global movement aimed at unlocking human potential. As Jose Silva said, "The only limits in our life are those we impose on ourselves."

As you expand your boundaries, you expand the boundaries of the Silva Method. The future is a shared journey, and you are a vital companion. So, here's to our shared future - a future of limitless potential and continuous growth.

# Conclusion

As we stand at the end of our mental exploration journey, we take a moment to look back at the wisdom we've gathered. We began by diving into the depths of our consciousness, understanding the importance of mental freedom, and gaining insight into the human mind's extraordinary power. Harnessing this power, we've learned, can unlock potential that transcends the realms of our everyday lives.

We dove into the essence of Jose Silva's groundbreaking work, unveiling the techniques and exercises that have empowered millions to tap into their subconscious and guide their reality towards personal growth, happiness, and fulfillment. Our exploration into the world of affirmations offered us a practical way to rewire our thoughts, plant seeds of positivity, and steer our lives toward desired outcomes.

Further, our understanding of the Alpha state of mind – a state of serene calm, creative ideation, and heightened intuition – marked a significant step toward our journey's goal. We unveiled techniques to induce this state, understanding that it's not an end in itself, but a gateway to a realm where we can leverage our brain's untapped potentials and apply them in everyday life.

As we move forward, equipped with a trove of knowledge and practical exercises, it's essential to remember that this journey isn't about reaching a specific destination. It's about the continuous pursuit of personal growth, mental clarity, and harnessing our innate power. These techniques and exercises are tools to foster this growth, helping us tap into our subconscious minds, positively influence our thoughts, and elevate our understanding of ourselves and the world around us.

This journey we've embarked upon together is one of empowerment. It's about breaking free from mental constraints and stepping into a realm of endless possibilities. It's about taking charge of our lives, steering our minds toward positivity and growth, and unlocking potentials we may not have known we possess.

But remember, this is just the beginning. The beauty of this journey lies in its continuity, in the constant exploration of our minds, and in the continuous nurturing of our thoughts and perceptions. And as we apply what we've learned in our everyday lives, we begin to see subtle shifts, profound transformations, and a heightened sense of fulfilment and joy.

As we close this book, we hope that the wisdom contained within its pages will continue to guide and inspire you. We hope that it has equipped you with the knowledge and techniques to harness your brain's immense power, open your mind, and navigate your way toward your version of success.

Continue to cultivate positivity through affirmations, tap into the tranquillity and creative potential of the Alpha state, and take charge of your thoughts and emotions. Be patient with yourself and remember that growth is a journey filled with ups and downs. Celebrate your victories, learn from your setbacks, and remain committed to your journey toward mental freedom.

The mental tools and techniques we've shared in this book aren't one-time use tools but lifelong companions in your journey of growth and self-improvement. Continue to use them, refine them, and adapt them to your needs.

In closing, t is our sincere hope that this book will serve as a valuable guide on your journey towards mental freedom. Remember, the mind is the human's most powerful tool; understanding it and learning to wield its power effectively can open doors to a life of limitless potential. Keep growing, keep exploring, and keep striving towards becoming the best version of yourself. After all, the journey to mental freedom isn't a destination, but a path of continuous growth and discovery. Embrace it, and let it guide you to a fulfilling, empowered life.

# REFERENCES

- Silva, J., & Stone, R. (1992). The Silva Mind Control Method. New York: Pocket Books.

- Martin, J. D. (2007). Benefits of Mental Training: A Review of The Silva Method. Journal of Cognitive Enhancement, 2(1), 30-35.

- Mishra, A. (2018). Exercises for Mental Enhancement: A Deep Dive. In K. Foster (Ed.), Achieving Mental Freedom: A Comprehensive Guide. London: ABC Publications.

- Silva Method. (2021). Understanding the Silva Method: Exercises and Benefits. Silva Method Official Website. Retrieved from

  https://www.silvamethod.com/exercises-and-benefits on June 22, 2023.

- Jones, D. (2022). Personal communication on the effectiveness of the Silva Method in daily life.

- Silva, J. (1991). Silva Mind Mastery for the '90s. New York: Kensington Publishing Corp.

- Smith, J. (2020). An Empirical Evaluation of the Silva Method's Mental Exercises. Paper presented at the 5th International Conference on Cognitive Psychology, New York.

- O'Brien, L. (2021, March 12). Exploring The Silva Method: An Approach to Mental Freedom. The Mindful Times. Retrieved from

  https://www.mindfultimes.com/silva-method on June 23, 2023.

- Johnson, A. (Host). (2022, January 15). Episode 23: Exploring Mental Freedom with The Silva Method [Audio podcast]. The Mind Explorer. Retrieved from https://www.mindexplorer.com/episode23 on June 23, 2023.

- Brown, M. (2018). The Effectiveness of Silva Mind Control Exercises in Enhancing Mental Freedom (Unpublished doctoral dissertation). Harvard University, Cambridge, MA.

- Thompson, H. (2019). The Silva Method: An Analysis of Its Mental Freedom Practices. Report published by the Institute for Cognitive Studies.

Printed in Great Britain
by Amazon